PRAISE FOR
Building Business Value

"*Building Business Value* forces owners and CEOs to focus on creating value as their first priority and then, with clarity, shows them the right way to get it done."

Paul Riecks, President, Inner Circle Mid-Atlantic

"I can tell you from my experience that many owners/CEOs do not seem to understand how to position their companies for premium value. Marty O'Neill has created a clear, easy-to-follow methodology that can add substantially to enterprise value."

Stan Sloane, CEO, SRA International

"Many books on related subjects present one or two of the ideas here, which causes business leaders to spin a wheel or two without traction. In his systemic and diagnostic approach, Marty O'Neill provides an essential tool for business leaders to accelerate the process of adding value to midsize companies—internally and externally. *Building Business Value* presents a way to move forward with purpose, not frenzy. I'm eager for my leadership team to read it."

Kris Kurtenbach, Founding Partner, Collaborative Communications Group

"This book should come with a highlighter and extended margins because of the tremendous amount of relevant information that prompts thought on every page."

Drew Hudson, President and COO, The Choice Inc.

"This work is like walking into an Apple store. My advice . . . pick something that resonates and use it—then reread it and pick another concept and use it in your operation."

Tom Morrison, Principal, Morrison Partners

"*Building Business Value* proves you can find gold in your own backyard."

Len Moodispaw, Vice President, Essex/Northrop Grumman

"Marty O'Neill's visionary book *Building Business Value* has captured the essence of defining and applying transformational initiatives within your organization, leading to enhanced enterprise value."

Leo F. Fox III, President, Tenacity Solutions, Inc.

"In *Building Business Value*, Marty O'Neill provides a useful and practical guide to business leaders in the small and medium business enterprise markets. This book is a must-read for sophisticated entrepreneurs who are looking to maximize enterprise value."

Gus Cicala, President and CEO, Project Assistants, Inc.

"As a founder and CEO of a midsized business, I have always known it was my job to create and build value. *Building Business Value* provides a clear road map of exactly how to do it."

David G. Walker, President and CEO, Pangia Technologies

"Ten years from now, this is what you'll wish you knew today."

Daniel L. Goldberger, Partner, Grant Thornton, LLP

"The book reads like a conversation with a wise uncle that connects with you just at the right time—when your own wisdom and maturity allow you to listen and appreciate the advice that can only come from a life's journey through the corridors of business."

Armando Seay, Cofounder, RTGX

"Marty has done a great job of laying out a step-by-step process for the CEO that wants to maximize the value of his company, which is frankly something that every competent CEO must do."

Paul Silber, Silber Associates (former CEO of In Vitro Technologies)

"*Building Business Value* forced me to reevaluate the factors that impact tangible value in our company. This book challenges business leaders to think bigger and look for the blind spots that can limit future financial returns."

Tracy Graves-Stevens, President and CEO, MSM Security Services, LLC

"I wish I had read this book ten years ago. Marty O'Neill lays out a realistic process for achieving what seems to many of us serial entrepreneurs to be a very elusive goal. I would be a rich woman today if I had had this extremely practical and entertaining book at my side."

Susan Stalick, Management Consultant

"Getting things done well is not happenstance. It is planning and execution, and O'Neill nails it again and again. Read this book and keep it on your desk. Better yet, make it a daily meditation."

Dennis J. Roberts, Chairman, The McLean Group

"Whether you're interested in positioning your business for sale at a premium price or just trying to optimize your operations and maximize your profits, *Building Business Value* can help. Drawing on his years of experience in running, building, and selling successful companies, Marty O'Neill provides a cogent road map for creating and maximizing value in any business. His model is easy to understand and apply. *Building Business Value* is written in an engaging style, replete with examples, charts, and checklists."

Laurens MacLure, Jr., President and CEO, RWD Technologies

"If a company is in fact a diamond mine but doesn't know it, it should read the book by a miner of gems. Marty sheds considerable light on the matter!"

Ray Dizon, Managing Director, Maryland Venture Fund

"In *Building Business Value*, Marty O'Neill makes a case for building value in your organization that no owner or executive will want to ignore. Marty's value-building strategies are supported through personal real-world examples and stories. Marty's insights have inspired transformations that added real value to Tenacity Solutions."

Matt Wilmoth, Cofounder and Vice President, Tenacity Solutions Inc.

"Finally! A systematic approach to achieving top valuations. A wonderful tool for entrepreneurs at any stage of development."

Ellen Hemmerly, President, bwtech@UMBC Research & Technology Park

"*Building Business Value* is a book that I wish I could give to all my prospective clients. Not only would it greatly improve the potential purchase price for these clients, but it would make my job much easier! A great resource for all business owners who recognize that their companies aren't going public tomorrow."

Gretchen F. Guandolo, Principal, Agility Advisors

"I have read many management and leadership books, but this one by Marty O'Neill gets immediately to the heart of the matter and provides concrete steps to increasing an organization's value. This book is both easy to read and a great reference book for creating vision and taking action within organizations."

John McBeth, President and CEO, Next Century Corporation

Building Business Value

How to Command a Premium Price
for Your Midsized Company

Martin O'Neill

THIRD BRIDGE PRESS
ARNOLD, MARYLAND

Third Bridge Press
1290 Bay Dale Drive, #323
Arnold, MD 21012
Tel: 866-584-5639   www.thirdbridgepress.com

Ordering Information
Quantity sales. Special discounts are available on quantity purchases by corporations, associations, and others. For details, contact the "Special Sales Department" at the Third Bridge Press address above.
Individual sales. Third Bridge Press publications are available through most bookstores. They can also be ordered directly from Third Bridge Press at the number above.
Orders by U.S. trade bookstores and wholesalers. Please contact Cardinal Publishers Group: Tel: (800) 296-0481; Fax: (317) 879-0872; www.cardinalpub.com.

Printed in the United States of America

Cataloguing-in-Publication data
O'Neill, Martin F., 1959-
    Building business value : how to command a premium price for your midsized company / Martin O'Neill.
        p. cm.
    Includes index.
    ISBN 978-0-9820569-0-5
    1. Success in business. 2. Business logistics. 3. Strategic planning. 4. Small business—United States—Growth. 5. Small business—United States—Management. 6. Small business—United States—Planning. I. Title.
HD62.7 O5   2009
658.1/592—dc22   2008911726

FIRST EDITION
14 13 12 11 10 09   10 9 8 7 6 5 4 3 2 1

Cover design: Bookwrights
Interior design and composition: Beverly Butterfield, Girl of the West Productions
Editing: PeopleSpeak

To Denise, Jack, Liam, and Lily

who continually teach me about what is truly valuable

CONTENTS

PREFACE

If you're like most leaders of a midsized company, you probably feel like you have one of the best jobs in the world. I've been in your shoes and have experienced many of the same hopes and fears you have. Most of the time, you would not trade your role with anyone. But there are times, probably more than you let on, when you hold what seem like contradictory positions that are virtually incompatible. For example, business may be going great, but you are always worried about the overall economy or maybe just your specific market segment. Or you now find your company is past the start-up phase, but you are still obsessed about the little issues that leaders of bigger companies should not be worrying about. You handpicked your leadership team, but you are still not sure you have the right team to take you to the next level. You feel like you are on the right track, but you don't have a scorecard to tell you where you really stand. You've had some success, but you are not 100 percent sure if you can repeat it. You know companies in your market are doing well, but you've convinced yourself there are valid reasons your growth is not where you want it to be.

It was this dichotomy that led me down the path of creating the value-building process I explain in *Building Business Value*. These contradictions made me wonder whether the leaders of my competition were struggling with the same issues and whether all midsized leaders struggled with these same issues. I also began to consider how large, publicly traded companies managed their way through these apparent contradictions.

While I was the CEO of CTX Corporation I really began to find the value of running our midsized company like a publicly traded firm. Not that I had to fret over Sarbanes-Oxley compliance, but I found that if I could run the company based on the collection and analysis of sound metrics and I could really find out what factors increased its value, then I could build initiatives that focused on those value drivers and let all the minutiae (that normally keep us all awake) fade away.

One more step our business leaders had to take to make this value-building process stick was that everyone who could influence the value driver had to buy into what we were doing. Sitting in an ivory tower and pulling strings (or analyzing financial statements) would not work. Each leader had to understand each value driver, the impact it had on the company, and specifically what needed to be done to move the value driver in the right direction.

This was the genesis of the value-building process. It is a leadership-driven, collaborative process that forces the executives of midsized companies to examine what is really important to their businesses. It makes you, as a leader of a midmarket company take an honest assessment of your company, paint a picture of where you want it to be, analyze the gaps, and then build transformational initiatives based on your company's current state, the value drivers in your market, and finally, a frank evaluation of your team's ability to execute.

You may be one of those business leaders who is a bit hesitant to go through such a process because you are not interested in selling your company or you are nervous about using the word "value" in front of your employees. As a C-level executive, your main priority and commitment to your company is to build value. If you are planning to go public in the future, you should be building value. If you plan to leave your company to your children or your employees, you should be building value. If you plan to run the company as a lifestyle company, you should be building value. If you are planning to sell today, tomorrow, next year, or five years from now, you should be building value.

Building Business Value is a book about process. My sincere desire is that any leadership team of a midsized company can quickly put to use the methods and tools found in these pages to create an actionable plan for building business value. I've structured the book according to the logical sequence of events for any planning session. There is a natural flow to successful business transformations, and the chapters follow that flow. Throughout the book I share success stories and anecdotes from previous work experiences as real-life examples.

I wish you the very best as you take your company on a value-building journey.

Martin F. O'Neill

CHAPTER ONE

Don't Stop Thinking about Tomorrow

The future has a way of arriving unannounced.
GEORGE F. WILL

Give me a place to stand, and I will move the world.
ARCHIMEDES

They say that your reputation is determined by the company you keep. But your wealth is determined by the company you sell.

Business owners make their fortunes the day they exit the businesses they have painstakingly worked to create. Whether they are selling their company to another business or to their own employees, or thinking big and going public, the ultimate paycheck—the one with all the zeros on it—comes on one momentous day. How important of a day that will be for you is a function of how much value your company has created. How you navigate the daily challenges between now and then can leave you feeling like you are defying gravity.

Most companies sell at subpar to par value, meaning that the ultimate price tag is somewhere between three to five times the company's annual EBITDA—earnings before interest, taxes, depreciation, and amortization. Poorly run companies sell for a smaller multiple, while companies that are run about as well as their average competitors might go for four or five times their net earnings. But just as superpremium ice creams command a higher price in the marketplace, some companies sell for a superpremium of nine to ten times net earnings. It's the difference between generic ice cream and Häagen-Dazs. So the questions are these: Why do some companies command that superpremium price while others don't, and if you are a C-level executive (CEO, CFO, or COO) of a $10 to $100 million enterprise, what do you need to be doing right now to prepare your business for your exit at a superpremium price?

Typically, this is the moment in the conversation when the CEO says, "But we're not going to exit today or tomorrow!"

That's not the point. You will be exiting one day, and the time to start preparing for that event is now. You have a responsibility to yourself, to your family if you intend to leave the business to them, and to your employees, shareholders, investors, and other stakeholders to maximize the value of your business. In other words, the actions you take today will determine whether your business sells at a subpar, par, or premium price. Since that's the case, why don't all business owners and C-level executives focus on value creation as job one?

Thinking Ahead

In my experience working as a C-level executive in a company that sold for an almost-unheard-of price of sixteen times net earnings and another that sold for more than ten times earnings, and as a consultant who has guided companies to hundreds of millions of dollars of value creation, the answer is obvious: *it's hard to think about the future when you've got so much to worry about today.* Most leaders function in an atmosphere of juggling crises. They step off a flight to 116 new e-mails and have to devote their most precious resource—their time—to figuring out what needs to be handled immediately, what can wait for a few hours, and what can wait until tomorrow. In today's hyperfrenetic business climate, it's all but impossible for leaders to indulge themselves in the ultimate luxury—uninterrupted time devoted to thinking about and planning for the future.

The typical solution for harried C-level executives is an off-site meeting, but such meetings typically devolve into extended bull sessions in which people utter a lot of high-minded, well-intentioned platitudes about the future but rarely figure out how to translate those impressive sentiments into action items. You know the feeling, that "off-site euphoria" you experience when you wrap up the meeting with optimism and energy. But that feeling is soon replaced by the harsh reality of the daily grind as the wave of missed deadlines, extended due dates, and lack of follow-through becomes apparent. The good news is that everybody gets in a few days of golf, but then it's back to the office, with nothing changed.

Another pitfall executives are prone to when thinking or communicating about the future is a lack of interest in conveying their vision to the rest of their team. Entrepreneurs and midmarket executives often play their hands close to the vest. They can have a difficult time trusting others with their vision of the future of the business. It's impossible, of course, to get people to buy into a future they know nothing about. And yet, all too often, business owners and CEOs keep their ideas about the future to themselves. This means that no exit is planned, which leads to subpar or par (at best) valuations when the exit opportunity finally arrives.

The fact that executives of publicly traded corporations have a stock price with which to contend is both a blessing and a curse. On one hand, they have immediate, minute-by-minute feedback from the marketplace as to how their enterprise is performing. The downside is the tendency to manage for the short term—to focus on the day-to-day stock price or limit "long-range planning" to the period between now and the end of the quarter. In contrast, no "stock market" exists for shares of businesses that are not publicly traded. The trade-off here is that leaders don't have to worry about satisfying Wall Street's expectations, but they often lack the market discipline that Wall Street forces upon publicly traded companies.

Without that discipline, and with the entrepreneurial tendency to hoard information or to indulge in freewheeling and ultimately useless planning sessions and off-site meetings, it's no wonder that few leaders ever focus on an exit strategy. Neglecting to plan this strategy may not be reflected in the day-to-day earnings of the business, but it can cost millions or even tens of millions of dollars at the ultimate reckoning—the sale of the business, the leveraged buyout (LBO), or the day the company goes public.

Most CEOs spend too much time on the details, like the subtleties of new benefits packages, instead of looking at the bigger questions of "Where are we now?" and "Where do we want to go?" They "stay in the noise." Instead, CEOs should be asking themselves what drives value in their company. They need to ask themselves if they are working *on* the business or *in* the business. If they spend most of their time *in* the business, they are part of the problem. They should be asking themselves what they would be doing differently if there *were* a stock exchange for midmarket companies. Most entrepreneurs are good at operating businesses—they're good at what they do. They know they need to make money, to satisfy customers, and to keep their employees happy. But do they know whether there will be a future for their products and services? Are they targeting the right market segments? Can they repeat what they've done in the past but on a larger scale? Anyone with some financial savvy will be primarily interested in the trailing twelve months. But the future is the sizzle. To command a premium price, it's not enough to have your rearview mirror polished to a shine.

If you focus on the question of creating value over the long haul, when it comes time to exit, you can command a superpremium price. The same steps you need to take in order to make your business more attractive to buyers also make you more money in the short term. They are the same steps you need to take to create opportunities for your staff, returns for your shareholders, benefits for your stakeholders, and personal fulfillment for yourself. There's no trade-off between thinking about tomorrow and operating wisely today. Chris McGoff, former CEO of Touchstone Consulting, reflects back to selling Touchstone to SRA International in April 2005, saying "the surprising thing to us was that building a company that is attractive to acquirers and building a company that is built to last is the exact same thing."[1] The goal is the same for both: always create *enterprise value* (EV) in everything you do. What is enterprise value? The term enterprise value is often used interchangeably with others—fair market value, total enterprise value, and market value mean roughly the same thing to businesspeople, although they have specific nuances for the attorneys. I use the term EV to represent them all. Let the lawyers worry about more specific language when it comes time to do the closing. My definition of EV is this: the amount a willing seller and a willing buyer will come to agree on as an appropriate price for a business. Whether that number is $5 million, $20 million, or ten times that, the transaction will be conducted based on that number. That's true whether the transaction will be in the form of an asset sale, a stock transaction, a sale to employees, or a public offering.

Refining Enterprise Value

EV encompasses much more than the book value or the assets of a company. The brand and many other factors drive value—not just the numbers that you drop into financial statements. Although your accountant and your investment banker might seek to determine the value of your business strictly from the financial statements, a business is far more than a snapshot of the balance sheet or an income statement's look at the past. When people buy your company, they certainly value it on past performance. What they're really buying, however, is your ability to execute in the future. That intangible is not a number that can be captured on a balance sheet. Instead, your acquirer will be examining your marketplace, your team, the question of how sustainable your product or service may be, your business development pipeline, and other factors. Your financials have to be sound and defensible, but if you want to command a superpremium price, you've got to be able to show in a legitimate and convincing manner that your future is even rosier than your present or your past.

To that end, rule one for the CEO who is aiming to get a premium price down the road is this: stop focusing on anything that doesn't add value. You can find a way to move beyond the "hair on fire" approach to management, the lurching from crisis to crisis that bedevils so many CEOs. Instead, formulate a recipe for creating premium value.

Six years ago, I went to work for a company called Conquest, which had started out in CEO and founder Norm Snyder's basement making software for the computer-aided software engineering (CASE) marketplace. Conquest, at the time, was Norm, a partner, and a desire to sell their software. Norm had no leadership team, no outside advisors, and no standard financials. He kept the entire financial life of the company on a single Excel spreadsheet, which he lovingly called "Bessie." In fact, when Norm describes this period of Conquest's corporate history, he calls it a "prescription for *slowth*." Are any of these familiar to you?

- Decide what you want to build, not what the customers need.
- Sit in a room for years writing software.
- Invest all of your money, including retirement savings.
- Work with terrific people who are just like you.
- Keep doing what you are doing and be confident that everything will get better.

After a number of years of struggling to make a living, failing to build market share, and eating a lot of peanut butter and jelly, Norm pivoted the company 180 degrees and turned the focus toward software services. He successfully shifted the company from a producer of software to an information technology (IT) services firm. The company experienced dramatic growth over about a three-year period during which Conquest saw revenues grow 133 percent and earnings soar 119 percent from 1999 to 2003. Sales revenue topped $100 million in 2003 with projections of ever greater gains in the coming years (see figure 1.1).

Norm had been my first boss out of college, when I went to work at Booz Allen as a consultant. After Norm left Booz Allen to build Conquest, we exchanged Christmas cards over the years, and when his company approached the $50 million mark, I decided to

Figure 1.1

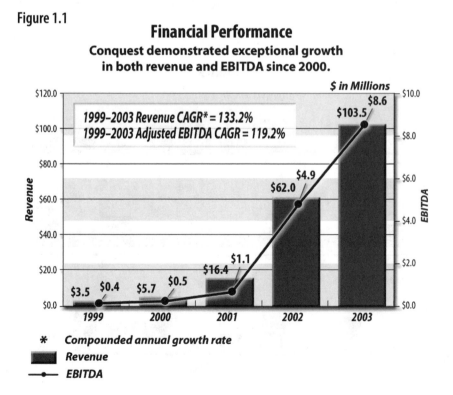

Financial Performance
Conquest demonstrated exceptional growth in both revenue and EBITDA since 2000.

1999–2003 Revenue CAGR* = 133.2%
1999–2003 Adjusted EBITDA CAGR = 119.2%

$ in Millions

* Compounded annual growth rate
■ Revenue
—●— EBITDA

join as COO-CFO. Norm's objective in hiring me was this: get the company's annual revenues from $50 million to $200 million and consider going public or even making an acquisition. The idea of taking a company public excited me, and that's why I signed on.

Life got strange in a hurry. I couldn't find cash flow projections or balance sheets. Instead, I found only Bessie, that mountainous Excel spreadsheet that Norm had been working off of all those years. The company did have a CFO when I arrived, but he left very shortly thereafter. The financial management team then consisted of Norm, our highly competent head of finance Lisa Snyder (no relation to Norm), and me. So we went to work modeling the competitors (see figure 1.2), trying to figure out how we stacked up in terms of SG&A (indirect and direct selling expenses and all general and administrative expenses), revenues, and net profits, and what we could do to figure out just what value existed in the "old girl." We began

Figure 1.2

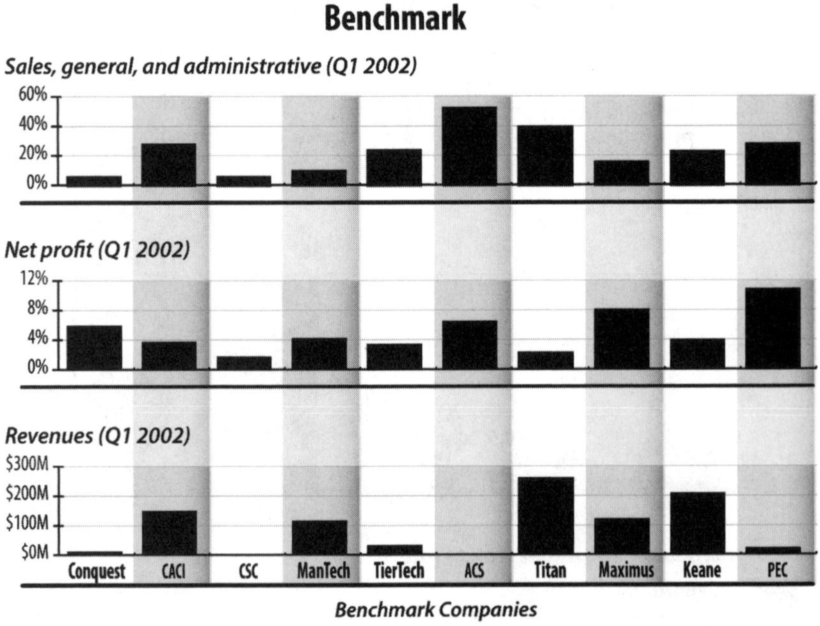
Benchmark
Sales, general, and administrative (Q1 2002)
60%
40%
20%
0%
Net profit (Q1 2002)
12%
8%
4%
0%
Revenues (Q1 2002)
$300M
$200M
$100M
$0M
Conquest
CACI
CSC
ManTech
TierTech
ACS
Titan
Maximus
Keane
PEC
Benchmark Companies

to benchmark our position with the competition; build a stronger relationship with our bank, Bank of America; create and document internal and governance processes that would pass any audit; and then determine the best place to use our assets.

When you think about the distant future, you think you've got a lot of time to make a plan. But I had been working at Conquest just three months when Norm announced a change of plans: he wanted to position the company for a sale—at premium value—within the next nine to twelve months.

Becoming Attractive

It was time to scrap the long-range thinking and instead start figuring out how to quickly position Conquest to make it as desirable as possible in the marketplace. We began positioning the company to make it look better on paper. Many of the company leaders were doing great work in their areas of responsibility but never really considered the fact that we might have to share our story with the outside world. As we began highlighting their successes, they all got their "fifteen minutes of fame." Paul Falkler, head of business development, had a great process and a wonderful record of winning business. We spent time documenting that process to show the marketplace that the company could sustain itself in the future. Kevin Reville ran one of our most diverse and entrepreneurial divisions, and we used that business to demonstrate that we were not overly dependent on one customer. Bill Anderson, one of Norm's very early hires and cofounder of their services business, was the "Culture King" of the enterprise, and we used the attributes of the workplace brand to show we could attract and retain staffs in a very competitive labor market. Kathleen Lally ran a very effective recruiting machine, and we highlighted those processes to prove we could continue to build our workforce over the next three to five years. Finally, we bottled the brilliance of our chief scientist, Carl Solomon, showing that we were actually ahead of the technical and market curves.

We then hired Grant Thornton International LTD, whose very fine partner Danny Goldberger began an auditing process, an essential component to any financial governance plan. The company most interested in buying Conquest was Boeing. Thanks to Goldberger, Boeing would be able to see audited financials—which is what its executives were used to reviewing—not a spreadsheet named Bessie. Boeing wanted to expand into our marketplace, envisioning the linking of its satellite business inside the Department of Defense with the kind of IT services we offered. We were a logical fit in Boeing's portfolio, and there were not a lot of companies out there like us. By the time Boeing came calling, we were up to $59 million in revenues, with projections to approach $100 million in a couple of years. Not bad for an entrepreneur, but barely a blip on the radar of a company like Boeing, a $50 *billion* concern.[2]

So we continued to find ways to make our company attractive. We created a financial management methodology and we highlighted our business development strategy. We captured and described in market terms the process by which we won new business to show Boeing and any other prospective suitors that Conquest would be a growth machine long after it was acquired. To get a premium price we had to demonstrate that Conquest had a lucrative future. To borrow Alan Greenspan's famous phrase, we needed to create some irrational exuberance about the company. The steak—the business that we already did—would earn us a hearing with the appropriate strategic acquirers. The sizzle of Conquest's future would be the force multiplier that would dramatically ratchet up the amount of money a buyer would have to pay.

We showcased everything we did well. We institutionalized the method by which we won business—we made it a process and a methodology so that we could prove to ourselves and convince other people it would continue. We needed to document that our ability to drive business didn't rely solely on the personality of key executives, which is often the case in small businesses. We needed to demonstrate that we had infrastructure and processes in place that would continue in the absence of the founder, Norm.

We drew attention to our market segment leadership—Norm had been around a long time and had done a great job building the business. Paul Falkler, our head of business development, had a terrific knack for winning business, but we built a repeatable proposal process that would long outlast Falkler's strength of personality in winning business. Others, like Bill Anderson and Kevin Reville, were pros at running their business areas. We simply had to bring out the fact that, although this was a young team, it was very competent and its best years were ahead.

We also drew attention to the talent we possessed. Carl Solomon enjoyed an outstanding reputation in the marketplace for his technology prowess. We made a big deal about Solomon in our presentation, and when Boeing bought the company, it made him one of its senior technology fellows, just one of sixty within Boeing's sprawling organization.

By the time we "went to market," the leadership team was aligned with the direction of Conquest, what our value proposition to the marketplace was, and how they fit into the overall strategy of the company. We knew where the company fit into the marketplace and the challenges we faced in going it alone and also what value we could bring to a potential suitor.

We used the graph in figure 1.3 as part of our growth and acquisition strategy. The figure shows Conquest's position in a unique market segment. Niche companies with little influence on the market are to its left, and large system integrators and aerospace companies are to the right. Conquest was the only company that was earning between $50 and $100 million in revenue in this market.

Figure 1.3

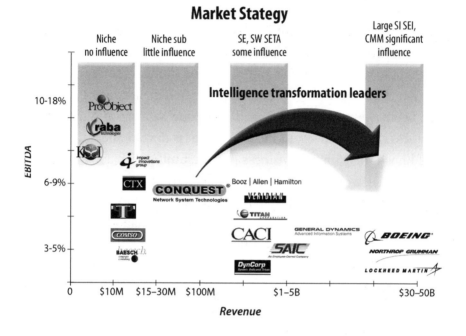

Conquest was well past the stage of a small business that could easily align itself with larger players and attack the market as teammates, but far from the size of the publicly traded competitors that had large business development and research and development budgets. This graph showed that we were in no man's land, and we were going to have to make a commitment to build through acquisition or look for the right company to acquire us.

Conquest's leadership wanted badly to influence the leaders of their target marketplace, which was the national intelligence (Intel) community. The only way we could do that in the short term was to position the company for acquisition by a potentially influential player like Boeing. Our belief was that Conquest's local market knowledge, teamed with a large aerospace firm's depth and size, would indeed allow us to influence that marketplace.

The National Commission on Terrorist Attacks Upon the United States strongly suggested that the national intelligence community needed to be transformed. This was no secret inside the community even before the events of September 11. Conquest leaders were passionate about their marketplace and wanted to transform the community. The team realized that the fastest and least risky way to do that was to join forces with a large player that had traditionally not been a player in the market.

We also developed a succession plan. Brad Antle, president of SI International (Nasdaq SINT), has acquired a number of companies in the midmarket. He says one of the major differentiators between midmarket companies and publicly traded companies is the midmarket's lack of solid leadership development and succession planning.[3] We produced and documented a clear plan that addressed these issues.

As Boeing evaluated Conquest, it was especially taken with our marketing "battle map." We knew our market segment backward and forward—where the opportunity was, where the competitors were, and where we would attack next. We demonstrated that we knew the marketplace better than anyone. We knew all the players, all the decision makers at a broad range of prospects appropriate for the business.

The point of all this was to make us the prettiest girl at the dance by playing up what we did well and downplaying (but never ignoring or covering up) the areas where we were not as strong. If we were weak in a given area, we fixed it. If we were strong in another area, we highlighted that.

Nothing we did at Conquest to prepare it for exit prevented the business from moving forward. The processes and methodologies we put down on paper made Conquest a better company in the short term in addition to making it a more attractive acquisition target in the medium term. Again, many executives are so focused on putting out fires that they don't recognize the squalor in which they are operating or their failure to make their environment better. They need to delegate better and they need to put appropriate processes and structures in place so that their company can sell more and grow more.

The work we did at Conquest allowed us to present Boeing with an extremely impressive package. We had a strong leadership team in place that would survive Norm's departure (and Bessie's, too) and we had a solid succession plan.

Our entire leadership team was clear about our mission, vision, and purpose, and we were all sold on it. We were willing to pay properly for talent, something that too many entrepreneurs and business owners are not willing to do. We had taken the time to think strategically about where we were going and had established our direction. We had aligned our constituencies and were motivating and inspiring the entire company to live one mission. Had we sought to impose those changes by fiat, it would have been fatal. Instead, we built consensus, so everyone owned the vision.

Under normal circumstances, Boeing would almost certainly have bought Conquest for anywhere from seven to nine times EBITDA, a premium price roughly double what a typical, decently run business in our market would receive. But the process of preparing for an exit did not take place during normal times. The tragedy on September 11 intervened, and since Conquest had a certain amount of national security-related business, Boeing ultimately bought the company for sixteen times earnings.

Achieving sixteen times earnings for your business would be a remarkable accomplishment and one that may be hard to duplicate, but if you follow the steps this book suggests, your business will run more fluidly and more profitably now, and you will be setting it up for that highly desirable premium price of seven or eight or nine times earnings. In other words, keeping an eye on the future will make you more money now and can double or even triple the amount of money that you will earn the day you make your exit. So grab a bowl of Häagen-Dazs or some other superpremium ice cream and come along for the journey to find your diamonds.

You shouldn't need to look far, as illustrated in a story told by the nineteenth century Baptist minister Russell Conwell. He dreamt of establishing Temple University although he didn't have any money. He didn't let his financial reality dictate his situation, encouraging himself and others with a motivational speech about a man who desired wealth so badly that he sold all his property, left his family, and set out on a lifelong, futile journey to find diamonds. He spent the rest of his years searching for something he never found because, as Conwell tells us, he didn't know where to look. Just after the man sold his farm, the new owner led his camel to water in the small river at the edge of the property. As the camel drank from the stream, the new owner noticed a flash of light coming from the bottom of the river. He knelt down and picked up what turned out to be a large diamond. After digging further, he discovered a whole mine. The man who left his family, home, and everything behind to look elsewhere for diamonds would have found them in his backyard if only he had stopped to look.[4] You can find the diamonds in your company too.

CHAPTER TWO

You Talkin' to Me?

If it fails, admit it frankly and try another.
But above all, try something.
FRANKLIN D. ROOSEVELT

Mistakes are a fact of life. It is the response
to error that counts.
NIKKI GIOVANNI

T he easiest thing in the world for an executive to do while reading a book like this is to say, "This stuff doesn't apply to me." Before you say that, take a look at this list of twenty-five mistakes that business leaders make that almost ensure subpar valuations when the founders or C-level executives are ready to exit. How many of these issues don't apply to your business? There is a test at the end of the chapter, so pay attention!

1. You have hired the wrong investment banker.

Investment bankers are in the business of making as much money as quickly as they possibly can. This means that most of them won't take the time to position your company for exit at a premium price. They're going to look over your company, figure out what it's worth on the market right now, and get the company sold as quickly as possible. The faster they sell your company, the faster they can pocket their fee and move on to their next sale. When Conquest sold for $80 million, the investment bankers from Bank of America entered the fray in September 2002 and closed the deal in February 2003. Using the Lehman formula for selling enterprises, which gives bankers 5 percent of the first $1 million involved in the transaction and a sliding scale down to 1 percent of everything above the $4 million mark, Bank of America charged approximately $1 million for six months of services by a three-person team. Running an investment bank is a lot like running a taxi—the more times you take a new fare and turn over the meter, the more money you make. If bankers view your company as a $5 million company, that's what it is. They're not going to help you position your company to become anything else. You want to make the most money when you sell, but they want to make a sale as quickly as possible. As the expression goes, "When the man with money meets the man with experience, the man with the money ends up with experience and the man with experience ends up with the money." Unless you've already taken your company to premium status or chosen the rare investment banker who will help you get there, forget about a premium valuation.

With the right investment banking expertise on your team when the time is right for exit or a liquidity event, you can become the man who has both experience and money. Good bankers give you honest information. They'll let you know if there is a market for your company. Good bankers will tell you when there is no market and a select few will actually help you prepare for an exit, even if it takes years. They understand that part of the work is transactional—selling quickly because the market conditions are just right. But they also understand that most midmarket companies should take months and even years to prepare for a premium valuation and profitable exit. Use the tool in table 2.1 if you decide to hire an investment banker. Interview a few bankers, rank them on a scale from 1 to 5 and see if they make the grade.

Table 2.1

Investment Banker Ranking

Criteria	Investment Bankers			
	1	2	3	4
Process				
Auction	2	0	3	2
Selective contracts	3	1	1	1
Confidentiality	3	3	3	3
Involvement of the officers	2	2	2	2
Involvement of staff	2	3	5	2
Knowledge of				
Investment banking (general)	2	0	3	2
Services lines	3	1	1	1
Primary segment	3	3	3	3
Secondary segment	2	2	2	2
Product lines	2	3	5	2
Other commercial buyers	2	5	3	2
Other federal buyers	2	0	3	2
Experience				
Banker's years of experience	2	0	3	2
Track record for like transactions	3	1	1	1
References	3	3	3	3
Team Strength				
Lead	2	0	3	2
Team members	3	1	1	1
Support team	3	3	3	3
Level of Service				
Conquest involvement	2	0	3	2
Book creation	3	1	1	1
Our involvement in process	3	3	3	3
Other banking resources	2	2	2	2
Wealth management services	2	3	5	2
Costs				
Fees	2	0	3	2
Score	2.5	1.7	2.8	2.1

2. Your business plans are ego driven.

Normally, a leader's greatest attribute is unbridled optimism. As retired General Colin Powell says, "Perpetual optimism is a force multiplier."[5] You would rather have Colin Powell lead you into battle than Eeyore, but you also need to deal in reality. The unbridled optimism that turns a business dreamer into a business leader has a downside: it can keep executives from confronting the hard facts about their organizations. Sometimes leaders sweep so much bad news under the rug that they can hardly see their own desks. A bright outlook is terrific, as long as it is tempered by an ability to deal in reality, a trait that not all leaders have.

3. You have "I'd like to thank the Academy" syndrome.

It's great when companies get awards—everybody feels good. The problem is that the red carpet fever can infect a CEO. When business leaders get awards like "Entrepreneur of the Year" or "Top 40 Executives under 40" or an invitation to the Young Presidents Organization or similar groups, they have an unfortunate tendency to believe that they accomplished single-handedly all of their company's success. This is a sure way to alienate the team. One suffocating ego is all it takes to destroy an otherwise successful business.

4. You have fallen into the "success trap."

In business today, things change so rapidly that what worked yesterday won't necessarily work today. But tell that to an executive who is so enamored of his own past performance that he can't see how the world has changed. For example, fifteen years ago, technical service companies could make handsome earnings by augmenting staffs to build custom business applications for clients. Today, however, those firms make a third of what they once did on the same deals. On top of that, clients expect that companies will outsource the technical services work to India and bear all the risk in the transaction. It's often tough to convince a CEO that what brought him success when Bill Clinton was president won't fly today.

Being flexible and blending new ideas with the old helps avoid this pitfall. Tenacity Solutions, a midmarket company in Virginia, has found a way to combine the old with the new. CEO Leo Fox says that Tenacity does business the old-fashioned way, and the company's staff and customers will vouch for that. He believes that serving customers and staff never goes out of style. COO Matt Wilmoth and Fox have built a company that makes great use of the "software as a service" business model and outsources virtually everything in their business that is not core to their reason for being in business.

5. You have "fat and happy" syndrome.

A CEO who develops a reputation as a turnaround specialist is likely to be wooed by other struggling companies to accomplish the same magic for them. To accomplish this, the CEO often tries to "put the band back together" by going out and rehiring the team that made the first turnaround so successful. The problem is that a lot of those executives may be fat and happy by now—they made their money on the first deal and no longer have the fire, the energy, or the desire to work those sixty-hour weeks again. Putting the band back together might work for the Eagles, but in the business world, people often end up singing an unhappy tune.

6. Uncle Joe's still chairman of the board.

The really good midmarket companies leverage their resources, including their boards of directors and boards of advisors. They use these business-savvy individuals as sources of wisdom and as sources of new business. John McBeth, a serial entrepreneur and CEO of Next Century, has a passion for what he calls a "worthy purpose." He keeps himself accountable by leaning on a top-notch board of advisors who aren't afraid to set him straight. In contrast to this, too many small and midmarket companies tend toward boards of directors that consist of friends and family. Perhaps Uncle Joe loaned the company $100,000 ten years ago, so he still wants to run the show. But friends and family who may have been able to pony up necessary start-up funds back in the day are not capable of providing the outside accountability that experienced business leaders offer. Many middle-market companies struggle with governance. Entrepreneurs and C-level executives need someone to challenge them and offer the guidance and direction necessary for growth. Uncle Joe may have great fishing stories to share at the board meetings, but he cannot mentor the leadership team when tough, challenging business decisions must be made.

There are other ways to fail to take maximum advantage of your board of directors. A company might have board members with personal agendas that lack transparency. Or a board member might try to buy the company outside the stated strategy of the executive team and the other members of the board. Leaders might isolate and disregard board members whose points of view differ from their own. That's why board diversity is extremely useful. Boards not only provide insight, advice, and support to the CEO, their members should have strong industry and financial backgrounds to add real value to CEO decisions. Board members not aligned with the direction of the company are harmful; those with axes to grind or agendas to meet must be culled. Outside directors give business leaders the opportunity to close the books every quarter, position their companies for the future, talk about plans and leadership development, and generally guide the company with the help of other experienced leaders.

7. You are focusing on revenue instead of value.

Middle-market CEOs often get asked "How big is your company?" In American business, size matters. Beyond the preoccupation with numbers and size is a much more important question that is rarely asked: "What impact does your company have in the marketplace?" Is the company a bit player, a role player, or the "leading man" in its market? Typically, business leaders describe their companies in terms of revenue, head count, or plants and equipment. Revenue is an easy answer because that's a scorecard everyone can understand. But when they use this measure, companies shy away from the "value discussion" because value is a much more esoteric concept. An exception to this rule is Ray Schwemmer. Schwemmer is the CEO of CollabraSpace, a midmarket maker of information-sharing software. If asked "How big is your company?" he always reports earnings. When pressed, he'll say that from a financial perspective, his focus as CEO needs to be on earnings—not revenue.

If the average middle-market CEO were asked, "What are the five things that make your company valuable?" she wouldn't know the answer. She knows her company has to make money, make payroll, and win more business, but she doesn't know what really makes her company valuable in her marketplace. This results in the tendency to make seat-of-the-pants decisions that are not fiscally prudent. A company might decide to sell a particular product in a market niche, even though no other company is willing to partner with it. Or leaders might decide to keep a line of business going, though it might be smarter to shut the line down and use the resources elsewhere. Know what makes *your* company valuable to the marketplace and what is core for you.

8. **When executives finally do talk about value, they drive everyone crazy.**

When C-level executives suddenly start talking about value, they often inadvertently strike fear into the hearts of their executives and employees. If value was never a consideration in the past and suddenly it's a big deal, employees may assume that the management is going to sell the company and they'll need new jobs. They may even respond by quitting. When you do bring up the idea of focusing on the enterprise value of your company, use the language carefully. You don't want people jumping off the pier just as their ship is coming in. Make "value creation" a normal part of your leadership vocabulary.

9. You have no conflict resolution skills.

Many midmarket companies are run by individuals with distinct competencies in a given area, for example sales, finance, or technical matters. Often these individuals are not experienced executives who have gone up through the ranks, so they don't always understand how to balance the competing—and they really are competing—needs and desires of the different arms of an enterprise. Some of these CEOs simply cannot handle the conflicts. Instead, they let them brew until their companies destroy themselves. If no clear direction is given, "ambiguity gaps" are opened. Failure to resolve disputes quickly and effectively is practically a guarantee that companies will self-destruct.

10. The bosses can't take a vacation.

At too many companies, the founders can't take vacations because they haven't figured out how to build effective teams, replicate themselves, or take other important steps in the value-building process. Sometimes it's not that they can't figure out how to build those teams—they just don't want to do so. Its important for leaders to learn how to let things go. Their resistance to this may stem from different root causes. They may have a deep fear that the company will go to pieces if they don't handle everything themselves. The identity of many executives is so tied up in their role in their companies that they have no idea how to back off, take a lesser role, or even leave. One company made an office in the building for the founder, who would come in and do nothing. It's extremely emotional for a business owner to watch someone else essentially rear his child. Letting go requires the ability to bring in new leadership and, when the time is right, to leave. But that's a tall order for most executives.

11. You are mishandling the communications of the corporate strategy.

You've got a new mission and direction as a result of your most recent off-site meeting. Great! Now how are you going to get the word out to your one thousand employees? Are you getting posters designed to illustrate your new mission, vision, or purpose? Are you stuffing paycheck envelopes with a document listing the five new goals of the organization? Most midmarket companies don't take these actions. If they establish a vision, the CEO fails to share it with others.

Other times, a CEO does try to get the word out but does so in a way that the Reverend Bill Hybels of Willow Creek Community Church calls the "Mt. Sinai approach" because Moses came down from Mt. Sinai with the two tablets denoting the Ten Commandments and demanded that they be followed.[6] That top-down approach might have worked for Moses, but it doesn't work in today's business climate.

Consider this from my upbringing on a farm. Cow paths make sense to cows. From a human perspective, the particular route cows choose for themselves may make no sense. But those routes make enormous sense to the cows themselves. People within organizations often operate in much the same way. They get work done by going to certain other people in the organization, regardless of what the organizational chart might mandate. If you try to impose a new structure from above without getting appropriate buy-in, you'll end up with two organizations—the one on paper and the real one. Executives in midrange companies often don't take the time to excite, coach, cajole, and mentor their stakeholders and their employees with regard to new structures, new directions, or new visions. They fail to do so at their peril.

12. Hey, we're making money!

Often managers focus solely on operational effectiveness instead of thinking about the future. The most effective middle-market leadership teams develop two paths for strategy, just as Conquest's did after deciding to sell the company. While the team planned for an exit, they also had to continue to run a great operation in case no deal was made. One path represents the present, and that's operational effectiveness. The other path represents the future—value creation. Losing sight of the future and focusing only on making an operation more effective now can leave a company vulnerable to major shifts in the marketplace. If your idea of long-range planning covers only the next ninety days, then this might be an issue in your organization.

13. You are not an S corporation.

If you're formed as an S corporation, you'll have options when it comes time for your exit. C corporations and limited liability company (LLC) formations may be the right formation for your company, but my preference is still Subchapter S. When Boeing bought Conquest, Boeing was able to write off everything that wasn't cash as goodwill. Both organizations made what the IRS calls a 338(h) (10) election. This is a fancy term you may want to study because it could save you big bucks. In essence, the election allowed Conquest to treat the sale of its stock as a sale of assets, paying tax only on the asset gain. Boeing, therefore, got a stepped-up basis in the assets of Conquest at a no-tax cost of the purchase and rolled part of that tax break into the premium purchase price it paid. Make sure your legal and accounting teams walk you through this because the benefits and burdens of a Section 338 may seriously affect the economics of a deal and may change your tax situation. The bottom line is that being structured as a Subchapter S gives you flexibility in structuring the best stock, asset, cash, or 338(h)(10) option for your company.

14. You only ask for money when you need it.

A company is only as strong as its banking relationships. A great banking relationship increases value by giving a company the flexibility to use cash when it most needs it. The worst time to ask for money, of course, is when you need it. You should sit down with your bankers monthly to tell them how great you're doing. You probably learned somewhere along the line that it is never a good idea to surprise your boss. Bankers are similar—they don't like surprises either. If they feel they understand the rhythm of your business, bankers are enticed to come to you with better deals, increase your credit line, and give you banking covenants you can work with.

Also with regard to banking, it's essential for the founders to get off their personal guarantees as quickly as possible. A founder should not be signing for a company by the time the company reaches the $10 to $15 million level, yet some $30 to $40 million companies still operate with personal guarantees. Founders and executives who are personally tied up with their banking relationship can cloud judgment, leaving their companies vulnerable to poor decisions on major investments. Large companies can easily use accounts receivable or other assets as collateral instead of personal guarantees for loans or lines of credit. Founders who are still signing personal guarantees are placed under unnecessarily high levels of stress, which makes their risk aversion levels higher as well.

15. Blood is thicker than water, but not necessarily what the company needs.

A family business can often be an opportunity to find employment for otherwise unemployable relatives. Managers of such companies tend to promote individuals they like or to whom they are related instead of finding individuals who are truly suited for the job being filled. This is not a good way to run a company. In his book *The Five Temptations of a CEO*, Patrick Lencioni says that when CEOs abdicate the responsibility of hiring, they ultimately lose track of their team.[7] Family members in the company place a huge burden on everyone involved and make it nearly impossible to execute good business decisions. Sometimes those relatives need to be taken out of those jobs to create a team that acts like a group of qualified professionals.

16. You have the wrong sales model.

Companies early in the growth cycle typically need direct sales forces—teams of individuals who are inside the company and know what's going on. While service-oriented companies normally rely on practice leaders (leaders who are responsible for profit and loss and have a vertical market expertise like telecommunications or energy) to sell, product companies normally rely on traditional salespeople. These are the bag-toting salespeople you see out there selling stuff. As the company develops a more mature product and begins to offer training, service, and other add-ons, it becomes time to change the channel models. For example, that's the time to get into affiliate marketing on the Web or build channels of distribution for your products and services that can leverage your mature product line. Yet many companies try to off-load their sales responsibilities too soon. A company's product or service may not be well defined enough to command respect in the marketplace, and the company may not have a support infrastructure to handle calls or complaints from customers, so all sorts of problems can happen. Practice leaders in the market still have a role to build relationships, and traditional salespeople may still be needed—not everything fits into an Internet shopping cart. However, close scrutiny of the sales model your company is using is important.

17. Any revenue is good revenue!

No, it isn't. Executives who feel that way are coming from a scarcity mentality in which they believe that if they don't scoop up every piece of revenue, regardless of whether it makes sense for the company, they're going to starve to death. They get used to selling anything to anyone. By contrast, an abundance mentality means focusing on a niche and dominating it. If a company doesn't dominate a niche market, when it comes time for the marketplace to put a value on it, the market won't know what kind of company it is. A prospective buyer will not be able to determine if the acquisition will be a good fit. A company needs to develop a sustainable market advantage, focus on that advantage, and brand itself in the eyes of its marketplace, or it is not likely to succeed.

18. We won, but we don't know why.

For a company to secure a superpremium valuation, it must show how it dominates a niche and sustains business in that niche. Far too many companies can't figure out how to repeat what they did well. When you ask their leaders how they succeeded, they have no idea. They rarely run a postmortem of their winning or losing bid with the objective of building a knowledge base of the lessons they learned. They also fail to perform what politicians call "opposition research." They don't know what positives or negatives people are saying about them or about their competitors. Typically, the last item added to a budget and the first item chopped in tough times is marketing, even though the information a marketing team provides adds value.

19. The wrong people are in the wrong seats on the bus.

In *Good to Great*, Jim Collins offers the outstanding analogy of having the right people on the bus—the best possible mix of managers, technical people, sales and marketing folks, and so on.[8] It's not just about having the right people on the bus: make sure that they're also in the right seats. As a former CEO, I have a degree in computer science and an MBA, so if you have great energy, I like you. If you are really working hard and have a great attitude, you'd have to mess up a lot for me to fire you. But as for salespeople, I can't read them. I can't tell who's going to be good at sales because the candidates all have great energy, at least in job interviews. Many CEOs who come up through the finance or technical tracks don't like salespeople because they are constantly making promises that the rest of the organization has to somehow keep. Brad Antle, the successful CEO of SI International, suggests getting your team involved so they'll be invested in the success of the new hire. Clarify the metrics of success with all parties so you can objectively assess your team. The challenge is to build a team who can hire the right talent even if you personally don't have the competency to recognize it.

20. You have misalignment of your core values.

Jack Welch once wrote that you can tell a company has reached maturity when you can fire the top salesperson for a breach of ethics.[9] In other words, if you're making so much money that you can afford to let go of your biggest revenue-generating employee because her ethical values are not consistent with the company's, then you're in a really good place. You have to be very clear about what your values are. This doesn't mean your company can't be diverse. Companies need diversity of thought and appearance to benefit from the broadest range of knowledge and opinion, but companies also need to be aligned in terms of values. One way to avoid misalignment of your staff with your vision is to be very clear from the beginning.

During the interview process or when making a selection for your inner circle, make sure you check the "alignment" box. Make certain each team member's values are aligned with the stated values of the company and your personal values (even if "make money at all costs" is your company's core value). At TiVo, the most important value is "creating a work/life balance for the employees."[10] Bringing a hard driving, make-money-at-all-costs manager into an environment like TiVo's would create a huge and unnecessary conflict.

21. You are owned by your customers.

Many midrange businesses depend on a single customer or a small (less than five) group of customers for the majority of their revenue. A lack of diversity in one's customer base hurts at valuation time. What if one of those customers fires you? Where would you be then? Along the same lines, some companies fail to manage their legacy products and never succeed at migrating their customers to new or next-generation products. The challenge is to balance diversity and focus with the objective to minimize your overexposure to one market.

22. You are still thinking small.

Recently, a company was considering the purchase of a second business that would double its size. The founder of the target company wanted to retire, and it was extremely important to him to find a home for his staff. The work of the two companies was compatible, and the target company's owner was ready to take the deal.

The deal represented a big risk for the buyer, though, not just financially but also in terms of his thought process. Excellence and comfort are usually enemies, and the owner of the acquiring company had to expand his thinking to accommodate a new enterprise that was double the size of his former one. Making this leap is not easy, and postdeal integration doesn't always get done. Take a look at AOL and Time Warner, Chrysler and Mercedes, or going back further in time, General Motors and Ross Perot's Electronic Data Systems. After an acquisition, it shouldn't be just one plus one equals two. It ought to be one plus one equals three—or more. A study done by the audit and tax consulting firm KPMG in 2001 indicated that in 83 percent of the deals they examined, the postacquisition value of the acquiring company didn't rise at all, and value degradation sometimes occurred when two companies were put together.[11] Mercer Consulting published another report in 2001 indicating that 50 percent of merger and acquisition deals actually reduced the combined value.[12] On the other hand, a Manufacturers Alliance study in 1999 suggests that CEOs consider only 11 percent of the deals they've done to be failures.[13] Business owners must have the courage to step up and make a strategic acquisition when appropriate, and they also need the skills to integrate the two companies after the deal has closed.

23. You're undercapitalized or overcapitalized.

For the most part, overcapitalization took place during the dot-com era. For example, a fiber company in Dallas had $50 million in venture money but never earned higher than $8 or $10 million in revenues and *never* made money. You should have seen its plush offices, though. This was in the era when companies routinely spent millions of dollars on image advertising during the Super Bowl and $500 a day on fresh fruit for their staffs. When the fiber company went out of business, it vacated some awfully nice offices.

If you're a sports fan, you may remember PSINet. It was the hottest Internet service provider during the dot-com era and even purchased the naming rights for the NFL stadium in Baltimore. Despite growing like crazy and being very well capitalized, the company was never profitable. It was a popular stock with analysts because of its rapid revenue growth and aggressive expansion plans, but by 2000, after its leaders spent money like drunken sailors, PSINet began to struggle. The company lost more than $5 billion in 2000 despite having almost doubled its annual revenues to $995 million. By the middle of 2001 it had built a debt of $3.5 billion and called it quits.[14]

The opposite side of the coin is undercapitalization. It's "business school 101" to know that an undercapitalized company is doomed to fail. But it happens all the time. Midmarket companies can find all sorts of ways to capitalize growth. They can leverage traditional banking relationships and turn to asset-based lenders. They can also create new channels and get their partners to capitalize their growth. One fast-growing consulting firm paid its employees a month in arrears. This took great pressure off its cash flow and allowed the company to expand into new markets.

24. You have no ability to scale.

It's ironic—few people plan to fail, but even fewer plan to succeed. Companies have great ideas for success but they never ask, "What if this goes well? What infrastructure will we need? What about collateral for the sales force? What kind of credit line will we need?" Companies need to be able to scale processes, people, technology, the product or service they offer, and methods of delivery. They may have beautiful numbers in their pro forma financial statements, but what happens when those numbers don't turn out to be accurate? In the 1950s, Leonard Wibberley wrote a novel called *The Mouse That Roared*, which later became a Peter Sellers movie. The premise is that a small country in Europe, the Grand Duchy of Fenwick, invaded the United States expecting to lose the war and receive generous foreign aid to rebuild. Unfortunately for Grand Fenwick, it won. Now what? How do you keep success from turning into catastrophe?

25. You fail to reinvent.

Tom Peters once said that we all have to "eat change for break-fast."[15] The only constant in the business world is continuous change, and yet many companies try to live in the old world and play by the rules that might have been in effect a decade or more ago. This just doesn't work. Have you ever tried to impose a hierarchical corporate structure on employees who are part of the demographic group referred to as "millennials" or "generation Y"? It's not going to work. A generation ago, employee attitudes might have been "We're going to win one for the Gipper," and "We'll stay up all night, if that's what it takes to secure the victory." Today's workers say, "Forget that. I just want to win one for myself." Any company trying to survive under the old model is destined for disappointment and heart-ache. Another example of this sort of failure is when a non-tech-savvy CEO says, "We don't need to be on Facebook or YouTube or MySpace. I don't even know anybody who goes on those places, aside from my kids." You know who goes on those places? Your customers do. Failing to keep abreast of changes that affect your business can set your company on the road to disaster.

So there you have them—twenty-five ways to doom a business to a subpar multiple come valuation time. Take the quiz in table 2.2 to see how prepared you and your company are. Once you've taken an honest look at yourself, you can begin the process of building a superpremium business value.

Table 2.2

Is Your Company Ready for a Valuation?

1	Do you have great financial advisors?
2	Is your business plan based on reality?
3	Is your ego in check?
4	Have you fallen into the "success trap"?
5	Do you still have fire in your belly?
6	Do you fully benefit from the advice of your board?
7	Is your focus on value and not revenue?
8	Have you had honest discussions on exit planning?
9	Can you manage conflict on your team?
10	Can you take vacations with relative ease?
11	Does everyone who matters know your strategy?
12	Do you think beyond monthly or quarterly results?
13	Are you an S-Corp?
14	Are your banking relationships strong?
15	Would you hire your entire leadership team again?
16	Does your sales model match your product line?
17	Do you dominate your niche?
18	Do you know your competitors?
19	Can you hire outside your personal competency?
20	Is your leadership team aligned to company values?
21	Is your customer base single threaded?
22	Can you build a much larger organization?
23	Do you have the capital to grow?
24	Can your company scale?
25	Can your company make big changes if needed?

How did you make out? Total your yes answers. If you answered yes

23-25 times, you're probably in the top one-tenth of 1 percent of leaders

20-22 times, stop reading—you're good to go

16-19 times, take this quiz again—and be honest with yourself

12-15 times, you're one of the gang—read on

 0-11 times, you're just like the rest of us—let's get started

CHAPTER THREE

Creating the Future

I shall be telling this with a sigh
Somewhere ages and ages hence:
Two roads diverged in a wood, and I—
I took the one less traveled by,
And that has made all the difference.

ROBERT FROST

The dogmas of the quiet past are inadequate to the
stormy present. The occasion is piled high with difficulty,
and we must rise to the occasion. As our case is new,
so we must think anew and act anew.

ABRAHAM LINCOLN

For centuries, Niccolo Machiavelli's name has stood for the concept of amassing power, often by nefarious means. He once wrote, "There is nothing more difficult to take in hand, more perilous to conduct, or more uncertain in its success, than to take the lead in the introduction of a new order of things."[16] His world was that of Florentine politics in the era of the Renaissance. It may have been easier for Macchiavelli to create change in Florence than it is for any C-level executive to shift the direction of a business today. Machiavelli could put his enemies on the rack or even get them excommunicated, and he didn't have to run his decisions past the head of human resources (HR). All CEOs have are stock options and the threat of firing people. Macchiavelli wouldn't have lasted ninety days in modern corporate America.

How exactly do you create a future that results in a premium price when it comes time to exit?

It's typically more powerful and more productive for companies to bring in outsiders to.facilitate this process. Companies that don't engage an outsider have no one there to challenge positional power. In larger, more established companies, a pecking order may restrict who can say what in an all-hands meeting. Sacred cows, land mines, turf wars, or whatever expression applies may inhibit a company's progress. An outsider can come in, eat the cows, step on the land mines, and conduct the discussion unencumbered by the ghosts of the past. An outsider can also introduce ideas learned from working with different companies. The process will go much more smoothly if you bring in an individual or team of people who can offer a fresh perspective and a point of view that is not influenced by existing company dynamics.

In a nutshell, the process is about identifying where the company is now, setting goals for where everyone wants the company to go, getting buy-in from all relevant stakeholders and decision makers, and choosing the three or four major focuses—transformational initiatives (TIs)—that will close the gap between where the company is and where you want to be. This process also involves identifying the basic improvements to operational efficiencies that will add incremental value to an organization. You've got to get those right if you're shooting for a premium price. Incremental growth is necessary but not sufficient to create a premium valuation. It's the foundation, and without it, a company is looking at a subpar valuation. The magic, however, comes when company leaders take a long, hard look at the company, determine the right direction in which to head, choose three or four TIs on which to lavish time and attention, and then achieve the leaps in growth necessary to build premium value. We'll start with a brief overview of each of these steps (see figure 3.1).

Preparation Time

First you need to recognize the distinction between outcome-based versus output-based action plans. Output is the hype that everybody writes down in a meeting. People throw ideas on a whiteboard, circle the best ones, and then go back to work, having forgotten everything that took place in the planning meeting. Obviously, not a lot of transformation comes out of a process like that. Instead of output, companies should focus on the outcome. The planning should

Figure 3.1

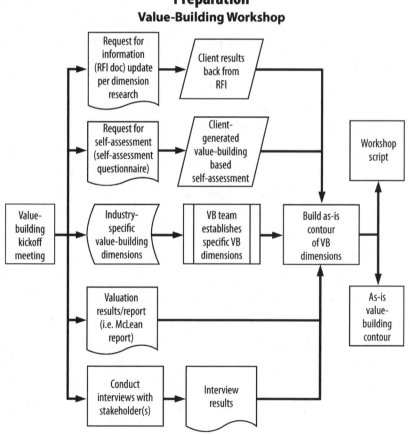

be based on the future, not the present or the past. You need to know what the target is—how big will your company grow and how soon? What new products or services will you offer? What new markets will you enter and what new opportunities will you seize? The goal is to create opportunities the company will pursue, as opposed to just talking randomly about where the company *could* go.

You can use this process in several different ways. You can begin to communicate where the company is going to stakeholders who can also begin to get buy-in from the various executives, decision makers, and other individuals whose opinions make a difference. Once everybody's in the room, you've got to get them agreeing about the basic questions of where the company is and where it's going. In other words, you're trying to find a way to communicate the company's new mission, vision, and purpose and get everyone on board.

How do you create ownership in a situation like this? How do you get buy-in to be more than just a cliché? A sense of ownership is created when executives are assigned tasks. Tom Morrison, an experienced turnaround executive formerly with Morrison Partners and now with Organic Alliance, uses a leadership concept he calls "share the vision." To make this work, Morrison says your leaders need to have judgment, intuition, and experience, and you must give them the tools and direction necessary to be a part of the action (see figure 3.2).

This method is different from the way Moses came down from the mountain with the tablets. Instead, everyone has a specific responsibility, something he needs to do, something about which he needs to be accountable to the board and to other executives. Too often, no clear connection is made between a function that an executive performs and the actual results that action creates. It's necessary to create a "line of sight"—a term Bob Blonchek and I coined in our 1999 book, *Act Like an Owner*—between what leaders do and the value of the enterprise. When executives have specific

Figure 3.2

responsibilities and clear lines of sight between their actions and the company's direction, you're on your way to creating a premium value. This also brings great credence to the process.

Step 1—Creating Commitment

To achieve true buy-in, start with the first step—creating commitment. To facilitate this process, you will need to understand not just the objectives and goals of your organization's leaders but also what's in their hearts. It's more than knowing a target date for an exit. It's about understanding what each leader really wants out of life. The following examples illustrate this step.

Chris McGoff, former CEO of Touchstone Consulting, wanted to leave the corporate world behind and start a consensus-building process for solving major world problems like immigration and global warming. He wanted to attack regional problems like shoreline degradation on north Chesapeake Bay and international problems as well. That contrasted sharply with the goals of many other executives, which often mean taking cruises and playing more golf. Those are perfectly admirable goals, but if the facilitator of the process doesn't know what all the stakeholders want to accomplish, it's hard to create a meaningful path to an agreed-upon future. Another executive with whom I worked, Rob Baruch, had a strong desire to get the University of Maryland Medical Center to invest in certain technology so it could be more forward thinking. Yet another CEO wanted to sell his company to a buyer that would take good care of his employees—allowing them to keep their jobs and make nice livings. He was interested in getting a generous payday at exit time, but he wasn't looking to make a crazy amount of money. The needs of his employees came first.

What do you and your team members want to do? Do you want to keep the company forever, make it a great place to work, make it a destination or a magnet for employees? Or do you want to sell it as fast as you can, take the money, and run? Do you want to be a pillar of the community or a fixture on the tennis court? If you don't get all of these desires into the open, you'll have executives operating at loggerheads while trying to create a new future. That's no way to get things done.

Committing to the process of transformation requires a lot of work and a lot of soul searching. Everyone has to stop and ask where she is, personally and professionally, and just as importantly, where she wants to be.

Step 2—Baselining the Enterprise

After you get commitment, buy-in, and agreement from the various team members, you can move to step 2, baselining the enterprise. To prepare for this part of the process, I give executives an RFI (Request for Information) survey.[17] My task is to get smart about the company. I pore over financials, press releases, business development pipelines, résumés of key executives, the Web site, and any other source of information I can get my hands on. I dig and dig and dig. I have a survey tool that takes about ninety minutes. In advance of the event, I sit down with each of the seminar participants, often by phone, and administer the survey to identify major disconnects between what the CEO says and what the rest of the leadership team believes. This kind of executive team surveying is all but impossible for an insider to do.

Step 3—Value Dimension Self-Assessment

Once everyone agrees on the baseline, it's time to perform step 3, the value dimension self-assessment. This spreadsheet outlines internal and external dimensions of value and components of each of those dimensions. The test lists ninety items on which to rate the company. The spreadsheet uses a 1 to 5 rating where 5 is best and 1 is the worst. The exercise builds consensus among the leadership team on where the holes are, on what needs patching, on what needs fixing on a basic operational level. Again, filling those holes doesn't take your company to premium value. But unless you identify and fill them, you're looking at a subpar valuation at best.

Step 4—Contour Map

After agreeing on a baseline, you and your team will create a contour map. The contour map was created by Brian Nejmeh of Instep Consulting as a way to visualize the dimensions of value. Figure 3.3 shows an internal contour map, with a cloud sitting on top of a multi-dimensional axis.

Figure 3.3

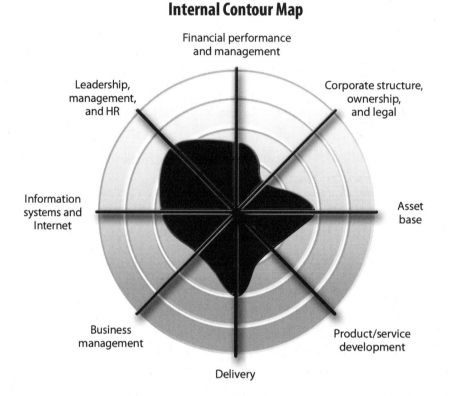

Internal Contour Map

If the rating determined from the value dimension self-assessment is weak, the cloud is close to the center. In the example of an external contour map (see figure 3.4), the cloud extends further out to the customer base area because the company is very strong in that area. The map is a visual representation of where the company is today and allows the leadership team to agree on the current situation where the company is. Sometimes I read the comments and opinions of different executives, and I think, "These people are crazy! They don't even know how far away they are from reality!" The contour map is a powerful tool for demonstrating exactly where the company is right now.

Figure 3.4

External Contour Map

Customer
support

Markets and
marketing

Customer
base

Sales and
channel
management

Pricing

Product/service
offerings

Step 5—Formal Business Valuation

Step 5 is a formal business valuation process. A company certified in business valuation is brought in to perform that formal valuation process. It reviews financial statements, merger and acquisition data in the marketplace, and any other relevant indicators to determine what market value the company currently possesses. This valuation is another tool for building consensus about where your company is at the present time.

Admittedly, all this isn't especially sexy. What you're saying is this: here's what we do, here's who we are, and here's how we think we stack up alongside the competition.

That's the preparation that needs to occur in order for the value-building process to begin.

Day 1

A representative sample of leadership with knowledge of how the organization works and the authority to make decisions now needs to meet in a cross-functional, facilitated workshop. That's business jargon for "put everybody important, no matter what they do, into one room, whether they like it or not." Together you begin to determine where the company is and where you want the company to be, taking into consideration what the marketplace is saying about the company, in order to begin to make it more valuable. Who attends? Everybody whose buy-in is necessary for change to take place. This may include the board of directors, leadership, the next generation of leaders, representatives of employees, and even, in some cases, customers and partners. If you want to get everybody on the same page, start by getting everybody into the same room. Figure 3.5 shows a workflow of what you'll experience once you enter the room.

When everyone's together, you can begin the process of increasing operational effectiveness, or the "elixir of strategic planning." This step creates incremental, evolutionary gains, which might include a 1.0 percent greater profit margin on sales or an increase of 6.2 percent in revenues. These gains put a little more money in everybody's pocket but add up only to incremental growth.

How do you make this kind of growth happen? Begin by using a tool called the organigraph, which was originally developed by Henry Mintzberg and Ludo Van Der Heyden of the University of Toronto.

As you see in figure 3.6, the organigraph shows how companies really work. It uses symbols like stars, funnels, tubes, links, and chains—in all, there are six specific symbols that represent how

Figure 3.5

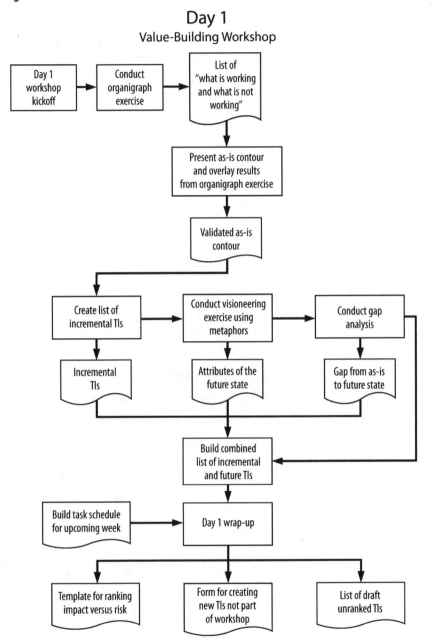

Day 1
Value-Building Workshop

a company really works. Organigraphs are a very useful way to show how a company works, showing critical interfaces between people and processes. Executives can use organigraphs to help choose among strategic options much as an explorer would use maps to find alternatives through rough terrain. The beauty of the organigraph is that it removes personalities from the process. It is "personality-independent." It's easier to embrace the idea of change if you don't feel personally threatened by it. Again, referring back to my early days growing up on a dairy farm, cows walk in goofy ways, but they know where they're going. Similarly, paper and approvals can take weird routes through organizations. The organigraph documents how companies really work.

The creation of the organigraph allows executives to draft a list of what's working and what's not, which in turn leads to the creation of a list of incremental TIs. Again, these increase operational effectiveness, which provides incremental growth and prepares us to take the next step, the visioneering exercise.

This exercise helps leaders visualize how to get to the place where the company wants to be. Linear-minded folks like finance people or engineers sometimes struggle with this, so have them draw images that paint a picture of the future. Typically, people will draw pictures of bridges, rivers, mountains, and even spaceships hurtling through galaxies to depict the direction a company is taking, the means by which it will travel, and what roadblocks and obstacles it will face. The exercise demonstrates some of the attributes of the future state of affairs, which everybody needs to see, because the company's not there yet! Another company created a graphic of the United States back when the interstate system was being built during the Eisenhower administration. Where was the company at that point? On the East Coast. The group knew they'd have to cross the Rockies, ford rivers, go through Indian country and other dangerous territories on their way to the Golden Gate

Figure 3.6

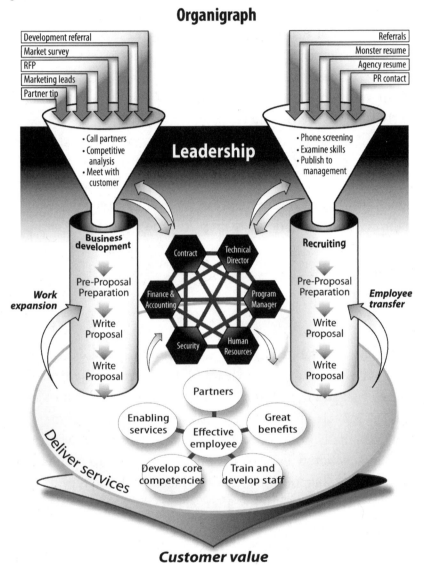

Organigraph

that symbolized the American West on their map. This didn't necessarily mean that the company was starting to market its products in California. It was just a visual metaphor for the idea of growth.

With a metaphor in mind, it becomes easier to discuss questions like "What does it mean to be nationwide? What does it mean to be global? What does it mean to have this new product set?" Somehow, a picture makes ideas more real.   .

The next step is gap analysis. Where are we compared to where we want to be? Now it's time to throw the net really wide and look at initiatives that are not incremental in nature but are truly transformational. Some ideas might be far-fetched. Encourage people to throw the widest net possible. And now, as day 1 ends, the homework for the attendees is this: determine which initiatives to choose.

Day 2

You'll notice in figure 3.7 that there is homework between day 1 and day 2. You and your team will be working hard to think through risk and return in order to narrow down the list of candidate TIs. Which TIs made the most sense? Certainly, some of the ideas presented at the end of day 1 are going to be too wild or too risky. So now you will measure impact versus risk to populate risk and reward evaluations of each TI on matrices. Leaders will be able to decide which TIs to follow, after seeing which ones offer the best ratio of impact to risk.

Companies should pursue no more than three or four TIs at a time. It's tough to handle any more than three or four. When executives say, "We've got seventeen things we're going to do in the next twelve months," they're not going to get anything done. It's the same as overcommitting to too many goals in your personal life. Identifying those top three or four priorities is critical.

Figure 3.7

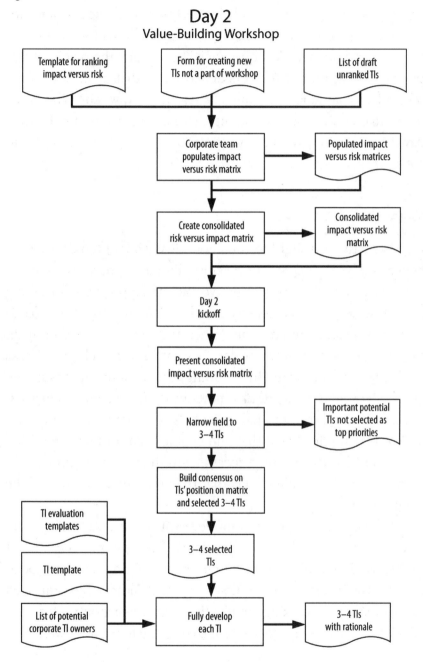

Day 2
Value-Building Workshop

It's not enough to have a transformational initiative as a catch phrase. Obviously, an action plan is necessary to make a TI a reality. It's time to sit down and create very detailed plans for each transformational initiative. Ask questions like, "Who's the owner of this process? What output is necessary to reach that goal? What's the schedule? What milestones must be reached and when? Who needs to be involved? What outside resources do we need?" By the time day 2 is over, you should have three to four highly detailed TIs to consider.

Day 3

Day 3 is actually a slight misnomer—ideally about ten days elapse between days 2 and 3. During this validation phase, two executives are assigned to each initiative and are responsible for taking the action plan created on day 2 and turning it into a full, board-level PowerPoint presentation. When the executives gather again for the validation phase on day 3, they have to sell their ideas to the rest of the team. In so doing, they build consensus, get everyone excited, make decisions about what the staff will be told, develop ideas about internal collaterals to promote the initiative, and receive the feedback that will enable them to fine-tune those TIs. Figure 3.8 depicts the process, with the teams of two starting with three fully populated TIs that they present to the rest of the team for buy-in.

Not everybody is going to love every TI. Structural changes can result in the loss of jobs, power, or status. A reorganization can result in the dissolution of a business unit or the shutting down of operations in, say, Europe or the Far East. Keeping the leadership connected to the problem by working through these issues as a group helps overcome territorial biases and allows the company to move forward.

Figure 3.8

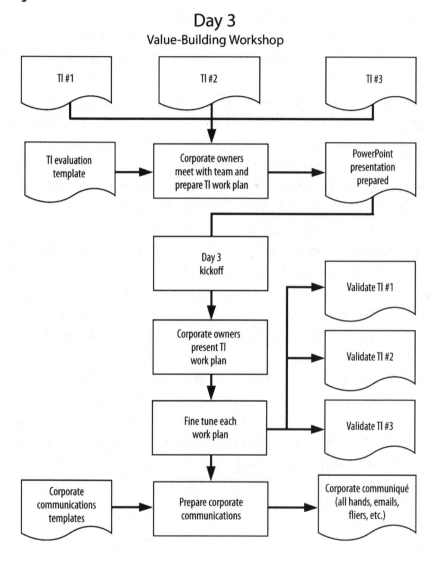

Day 3
Value-Building Workshop

People simply aren't comfortable with change. Change is hard sledding, as is the commitment of leadership to change. Why wait ten days to have these board-level presentations of TIs? Because everybody's got to get comfortable with what's been decided. If the CEO is not on board, he could shoot one or more of the TIs down immediately, and all that work would have been for naught. By giving people ten days to digest what went on in the first two days of the process, each leader gets time to say, "Did I really want this? Is this what I was really thinking? Is this what I wanted to happen?" It gives everyone a chance to say, "This is crazy. We're not going in this direction." Or, conversely, "This feels exactly right."

By the time day 3 is over, the three to four TIs selected on day 2 have been presented, debated, argued, and either settled on, modified, or shut down. The company now has a clear vision of its future, of what it needs to do to create both incremental and transformational change, and a clear road map that everyone has bought into. In other words, you've planned the work, so it's time to work the plan.

Sounds easy? Of course it's not as simple as throwing a bunch of ideas on a whiteboard, sleeping on it, waiting ten days, sitting through some PowerPoints, and making some decisions. This is the overview. Its time to get into the nuts and bolts of how all this actually happens so you can make premium value not just a pipe dream but a reality.

CHAPTER FOUR

Taking Stock

I can teach anybody how to get what they want
out of life. The problem is that I can't find anybody
to tell me what they want.

MARK TWAIN

It doesn't work to leap a twenty-foot chasm
in two ten-foot jumps.

AMERICAN PROVERB

Before you can build value, you need an honest assessment of your business. This is accomplished by collecting all kinds of data and conducting interviews with the leadership team. This helps establish where the organization is right now, but it does more than that. It keeps alive or reinvigorates the acres of diamonds that are inside your company. Not only is it about facing the reality of your business, warts and all, it's about ensuring that everyone is dialed in to the idea that adding value strengthens the company, secures more jobs, and makes it easier for everyone to make more money.

The process of gathering information is comparable to assembling your résumé or preparing your home for sale. You see where the gaps are—you pay attention to items that normally are ignored. You end up seeing the company in a different way, automatically gaining insight. This due diligence process gives people a chance to look in the mirror. Executives and employees begin to see how a coordinated, collaborated effort like this can lead to positive results.

You can get the whole leadership team involved in understanding where your company is right now.

Ultimately, this information becomes the basis for all the sound decision making that will take place over the course of the next year. Without this data, decisions are less sound and more seat-of-the-pants, which may be how entrepreneurs run their companies, but it's hardly a recipe for adding value.

John Cleese, the fabled television comedian, makes business videos through his company Video Arts. He speaks of Tommy the Tomahawk Missile, a smart weapon that can adjust in midflight, to depict how companies need to make midcourse corrections. That's a good metaphor for a company whose leaders can understand accurately and quickly where the company is and how it needs to make changes quickly. Those adjustments make the difference between par and premium value.

The next step in the process will tackle some of the key issues a company needs to address. Whether you go through this process in-house, with an outside facilitator, or in the quiet recesses of your mind (not recommended), be honest.

Gathering the Information

As you gather the information you'll be using for this process, if you don't have some numbers or a particular document, don't create them. I've found that some organizations just can't bear not having the answers, like the grade-conscious kid who can't bring himself to turn in his test unfinished, even though the teacher said, "Pencils down." Some companies operate under an ethos that says, "If you don't have the right answer, lie, or you'll get fired because you told an unpleasant truth." This process, when conducted by an outsider, can reveal an organization's ability or inability to tell the truth about itself.

When I worked as a business unit lead for a Fortune 100 company, monthly reports required a red/yellow/green self-grading process. Red meant trouble, yellow meant potential danger, and green meant all was well. This drove me crazy because the culture of my division was such that if you graded yourself red in any area, you might as well be updating your résumé because you'd be gone in months. Since no real information was getting through to it, management was unable to make timely decisions to fix problems. People were too afraid to speak up. One of the first things this process reveals is whether the organization has a commitment to telling the truth. It also helps facilitate the process down the road, determine what's broken, and decide what needs to be fixed to increase enterprise value.

The process is similar to the one a mergers and acquisition or valuation team would kick off if they were seeking to find a value for your company.

You can start with the basics. It's amazing how many midmarket companies don't have organizational charts. In the dot-com era of the 1990s, when everyone from lawyers to janitors owned stock, organizational charts and titles became passé until people realized they couldn't organize anything more complex than a company softball team without an organizational chart in hand. Does your company have an organizational chart? Is it accurate and up-to-date? Does it truly reflect how your company operates?

You will need to look at stock options, tax returns, and other basic documents that indicate your company's financial health. Does your company have audited or reviewed financials? If not, that's a potential sign that your company is not as mature as you think (or hope) it is. Many companies won't engage in the process of completing audited or reviewed financials until they are ready to sell. The audits and reviews can be expensive and time-consuming, but if you don't do them now, you'll have to go back and do them later anyway.

You've got to have an outside firm validating your financial reports and giving an opinion. Buyers are never comfortable with the books of companies they target unless the financial statements have been reviewed or audited by outsiders. Prospective buyers don't know how competent the internal people are.

The breakdown of equity is another area to examine. You may have equity doled out in many rounds of financing and in the hands of many angel investors, and that's a problem. It makes building consensus on picking a direction virtually impossible because different investors have different objectives. If one person owns the whole company, that's easy. If a hundred people each have a piece of the pie, that's a mess.

Do you know what your key management indicators, or KMIs are? You can call this group of metrics your dashboard. Well-run companies have really good KMIs. You can also review, as benchmark data, the KMIs of publicly traded companies in your market. What do they manage that you don't? Are you making forecasts on revenues and earnings and keeping track of trailing numbers over the last few years? Your competitors are.

Take a look at your banking relationships. As mentioned, mid-market companies need to get away from personal guarantees. They ought to have mature banking relationships, lines of credit, and enough money to perform operations in good and bad times. Where is your company in regard to cash flow and banking relationships?

Next let's now turn to staff issues. What's your head count? What kind of experience does your staff have? Are employees difficult to replace or supplement in your field of operations? Are you trying to hire very skilled engineers? What kind of education do you need your employees to have?

What sort of contracts does your company have? Are you the prime contractor or a subcontractor? Are your contracts long-term or short-term? Are they fixed price or flexible?

Get a handle on the intellectual property your company owns. What do you have? Did you secure it through patents or trademarks? Does your intellectual property make you special or different in the marketplace? Does it constitute your company's "special sauce"? Acquisition targets are infinitely more attractive and valuable when they have something special that sets them apart in the marketplace. Sometimes it's the intellectual property.

Sometimes it's the customer base. How do you view your market? Who's the competition? How big is your market segment? How are your leads initiated? Do you have a mature demand creation process? Not a lot of midmarket firms can create demand on their own. Only companies with a great niche or big companies can do that. Midmarket companies are typically add-ons—really good at following the leaders in a specific market. If you can create your own demand, you are way ahead of the game. Do you create demand or follow the market leaders?

How do you go to market? What literature do you use? What's your customer-capture model? Do you sell by relationships or needs? How do you market features and specifications? What's your sales model? Lots of companies have the wrong sales model for their products or services.

Do you sell to early adopters and innovators? How intimate are you with the scientists, engineers, or presidents of your corporate customers? Sometimes companies stay in the hand-selling mode too long and can't commoditize their product and can't get market share. Or they try to break out too soon, and their market is too much of a niche to become a commodity. Where does your company fall on this spectrum?

Is there alignment between what you sell, your customers, and your go-to-market mechanism? Are you using the right channels of distribution?

Where Do You Fit?

Next, it's critical for you to know where your company fits in the market. You can contact companies like Gartner Group, Fredonia Group, or Forrester Research to purchase information about your market sector. If you want to recapitalize or sell, you must convince people in the market that you're in a hot market. And if you want to sell, what's going on in your marketplace from a merger and acquisition standpoint? What are the terms of the deals being made? Are they in stock or cash? Who are the buyers—is the private equity market hot in your business space? Are all types of buyers interested or just strategic buyers? Are deals "bolt-ons," where a company wants to extend its reach by buying a competitor that performs the same functions in a city outside its current region? What's the churn—are there a lot of deals going on in your space, or just a few?

You'll want to focus on your company's products and services. What exactly do you do? What are your current product or service offerings? Are you in a changing market, a burgeoning market, or a dying market? How does the trendline from sales look—smooth or hilly? It's great that your company can make ten sales a year at $3 million per deal, but the market may be happier with a company that can do thirty deals at $100,000 each or three thousand at $1,000 each. This demonstrates a higher level of repeatable business.

After you've thought through your services and products, think about your delivery methodology. How long does it take to get a product to market? How do you support your customers and clients? Do you engage all of your customers the same way, looking like old-school IBM guys or Best Buy's Geek Squad? Or do all of your service-team people have their own look and their own way of working? Does your customer know what to expect when someone comes out to see her? In other words, have you made a science of service delivery, or are you still in "art" mode, where no two service calls come out the same way?

Next, pinpoint who your partners and your potential partners are.

What's your win/loss percentage on sales calls? Conquest won seventeen out of nineteen proposals in a two-year period. The marketplace loved that. We had battle maps, color-coded organizational charts of our customers—everything we needed to close deals and write winning proposals. This gives great confidence to an acquirer because you can replicate your business over time.

Now, go over your company's financials. You want to slice and dice them as best you can. Where are you making money? What are your gross margins? What division or business unit is making money? In what region of the country are you most successful? What product or service is contributing the most to your earnings? Where are you losing or wasting cash?

Turning to your organization's talent, who are your leaders? What are their biographies? Does their past experience align with their current responsibilities? What have they written or published? Are they well-known or even icons in your industry? Are the senior people patent holders?

Do you have succession plans in place? If you do, congratulations—you're a step ahead of most midsize companies, most of which do a poor job of succession planning.

These questions are the highlights of the RFI presented to leadership teams. Ironically, all company leaders have access to their own information and most have market data and some information about their competitors, but few use any of this information, whether already in hand or readily in hand, to their advantage.

What Do You See?

If you answer these questions, you will create a brutally honest assessment of where your company is. Not everybody likes to look in the mirror! Founders have emotional attachments to their companies that often transcend the need to see clearly what is going on. The habit of seeing through a gauzy film is a tough one to break.

If you go through all of these questions and you don't like what you see, don't be discouraged. It's still just the beginning of the journey. The next phase is to get to know the leadership, or for the leaders of the company to take a closer look at exactly who they are, what they wanted when they started the business, how close they are to achieving their visions, and how they feel about the future. But before you start asking them questions, you'd better find some answers yourself. Start by asking, Why did I start this enterprise in the first place?

I know why I started my businesses twenty-some years ago. I was at Booz Allen and had just finished my MBA and therefore figured I was the smartest guy in the room—any room! I had just put together a business plan relating to light industry in the area stretching from Camden, New Jersey, to Baltimore, Maryland. The first two partners to whom I pitched the plan hated it. The third one seemed to fall in love with it.

He then called a meeting, and he was briefing with my slides! My acetates!

I was so naive I sat there thinking, "This is great!" Any minute, I knew he'd say, "And Marty O'Neill's gonna lead this effort!"

My name never even came up.

I'm still not sure why I was invited to the meeting. The partner ran with the project, and I was never credited or involved. I was befuddled—until I realized that in the culture of that company, it was legitimate for senior partners to steal ideas.

Obviously, I had to get out of there, and that's why I went into business for myself.

Getting to Know Yourself

What about you? What prompted you to start your business? Or what prompted the founders of the enterprise where you work to create the company?

There are still more questions to ponder: How did the business evolve—what made it different over time? Is it still fun to operate? What do you like about it? Are you lonely and tired from over-work? Do you miss your family? Sometimes when people have been too long at the tiller, they begin to neglect parts of their business that are critical. What, if anything, is your management team not overseeing?

Sometimes looking at the aspects of your business that you don't like can give you insights about what you want. I've worked with an executive who was amazing in front of a group of three hundred but miserable if he had to meet one-on-one with anyone in his office. If he could have had a trapdoor behind his desk so he could avoid talking to any other human being on his way out of the building, he would have used it every day. On another occasion, I asked the president of a twelve-year-old, $15 million high-tech professional services company what he liked best about running the show. He responded, "Monthly employee lunches." Nothing else, just the lunches! In a company that requires customer intimacy for long-term success, the leader avoided meeting with customers and partners and only found satisfaction with friendly chat sessions with employees. So the question arises: what parts of your day generate a passionate response for you?

If the transformational initiatives are going to work, you've got to consider what the founder, CEO, and other executives really want out of life. Let's say that in order to receive the premium valuation someday, you and your leadership team would have to be employees of a loathed rival for three years. What if they couldn't do that?

To get a handle on what each person wants, ask him these key questions: What do you want to do in the future? What do you think your purpose is in life? What are you supposed to be doing? Everyone has a different response to these questions, ranging from earning a paycheck to taking care of his family, from doing great deeds in the world to feeling responsible for sending each employee's child to college. We all have different concerns that scare or upset us, from the price of gasoline to war in the Middle East. And we all have different responsibilities that require a great deal of focus and time away from the office, such as a child with special needs or aging parents. All of these issues must be considered when you are assessing your management teams and the motivations and distractions that drive them. Each individual maintains a unique balance between business thought and personal thought and corporate activities and the human aspects of his days. How do you strike a balance between what you would like to do at work and what you must do in other areas of your life?

Finally, at this stage, you should consider spending the approximately $8,000 to $10,000 it costs to have a formal preliminary valuation done. The McLean Group is one of many good companies that can help you find your value. An outside company like this should state your enterprise's value as a range. It's an important part of baselining. You might think your company is worth $100 million, while an objective outsider says, "No, it's more like $50 million." That's valuable information, and at that price, it's a relative bargain.

By working through these questions or the complete RFI, you have now come to a deeper understanding of where your company is, where your management team is, how the world thinks of your company, and what you have to improve in order to enhance your company's enterprise value. Now it's time to start thinking about what to do with all this great information.

CHAPTER FIVE

Agreeing on Reality

Reality is merely an illusion, albeit a very persistent one.

ALBERT EINSTEIN

I believe in looking reality straight in the eye and denying it.

GARRISON KEILLOR

Evaluating how well your company is doing today will provide an important baseline in the value-building process, and it will also help you build a strong leadership team. Your team is one of the keys to a successful analysis of your company's current position in the market, and it will be crucial in increasing your company's value. While this evaluation takes hard work, the benefits of having a cohesive leadership team that agrees on the current position of the company are priceless.

Stanton Sloane, the CEO of SRA International, has done six acquisitions in three years. Sloane said that on average, he and his merger and acquisition team sort through about a hundred "frogs" before he finds one company that's a "prince."[18] The hundred frogs are the companies that receive a subpar or par valuation. The prince is the one company in a hundred that commands the elusive premium value because it's doing the hard work that the other companies in its space are not.

But before you can start thinking about the transformational initiatives that will take your enterprise from where it is to the place where it can command the highest premium, you've got to talk seriously with company leaders about where your company is right now. You need to get everybody's perceptions of the company as it exists today out on the table.

This discussion will provide three immediate benefits. First, you'll develop a baseline, a market position that will make all of you nod your heads and say, "Yes, that's where we are." Second, this is the first step toward determining what kind of TIs your company needs to undertake to create a premium value.

The third benefit is the most important—it helps to connect people across the entire company. Enterprises rarely have company-wide discussions about what's really happening on the ground. For example, your marketing people may seldom have any contact with the folks in engineering, and your sales force may rarely have any meaningful interaction with the people in corporate planning. This exercise gives everybody a chance to have the kind of enterprise-wide conversation that almost never happens. Just getting the key players to talk about the same issues will be beneficial.

To help you get the discussion started, use the dimensions listed in table 5.1 to score your company on important enterprise value drivers. The table shows fourteen business dimensions divided into internal and external categories.

The eight internal dimensions are financial performance and management; corporate structure, ownership, and legal; asset base; product/service development; delivery; business management; information systems and Internet; and leadership management, and human resources. The six external dimensions are markets and marketing, sales and channel management, product or service offerings, pricing, customer base, and customer support.

Each dimension can be further broken down into six to ten areas that are more granular looks at each dimension. The term *dimension* takes on stronger meaning when you work with the contour map later.

First you will define each of the eight internal dimensions listed in the left-hand column of the table. If you feel your company has

Table 5.1

Enterprise Value Drivers

Value-Building Dimensions	Areas										Score
Internal	1	2	3	4	5	6	7	8	9	10	
Financial performance and management	2	0	3	2	3	3	3	1	1	3	**2.1**
Corporate structure, ownership, and legal	3	1	1	1	1	1					**1.3**
Asset base	3	3	3	3	2						**2.8**
Product/service development	2	2	2	2	2						**2.0**
Delivery	2	3	5	2	2	4					**3.0**
Business management	2	2	3	2	2	2					**2.2**
Information systems and Internet	3	3	3	2	2	3					**2.7**
Leadership, management, and HR	3	3	4	3	4	2					**3.2**
Dimension a											
External											
Markets and marketing	3	4	4	2	1	2	2	2	2	2	**2.4**
Sales and channel management	3	2	2	3	1	1	4				**2.3**
Product/service offerings	3	3	3	2							**2.8**
Pricing	2	3	4								**3.0**
Customer base	4	4	4								**4.0**
Customer support	4	2	2								**2.7**
Dimension x											
Dimension y											

Score each cell 1 to 5 according to the following scale:

1 - Area undefined, unknown, incomplete

2 - Underperforming, unclear, not mature, start-up

3 - Industry standard, compliant, meets expectations

4 - Above average, exceeds standards

5 - Far exceeds industry standards, surpassing stretch goals

additional dimensions to rate, you can add them to the worksheet where the placeholder "dimension a" appears on the worksheet. Then everyone will rate the company as a whole with regard to these dimensions. If you enlist the help of a facilitator for this discussion, remember that the facilitator will not tell you how your company is doing. That's something you already know.

Focusing on Your Company Strengths

Business leaders often ask if a company has to excel in all fourteen dimensions to build a premium value. Absolutely not. You've got to meet industry standards in each category (a rating of 3 on the scale), and you have to excel in the dimensions where your company has special expertise. Marcus Buckingham, who developed a "strengths management" approach to building efficiency, offers the analogy of responding to a report card your child brought home with three As, one B, one C, and one D. Which subject gets your immediate attention? If you're like most parents, it's the one with the D. Buckingham suggests that you focus on your child's strengths instead. Your son may be a prodigy in the subjects in which he received As. Get some help to pull up the lower grade, but don't waste all your time getting that D to a B or an A while risking the As.

Similarly, it is important to keep some perspective as you achieve an honest assessment of your organization. Eventually, you'll hone in on your company's strengths and bring your D grades up enough to stay out of hot water. The following examples show how this strategy can work.

If you've ever gotten a speeding ticket, then you've experienced the Doppler system of technology: it's what makes radar speed guns work. The man who invented Doppler radar is Harry Smith, and he's now in his eighties.[19] He's not exactly spending his retirement on the golf course, though. He recently invented a technology that improves signal-to-noise ratio on cell phone calls. If you're not a techie, that may not sound all that important or interesting, but this technology can improve the quality of cell phone calls and reduce the number of dropped calls.

Smith has formed a new company called Apex Eclipse to license his software to cell phone service providers like AT&T and Sprint in the United States and other providers in China, Europe, and all over the world. His company has to be extremely careful when it comes to protecting its intellectual property (IP). If somebody can reverse-engineer what Smith did, his company has nothing. So IP protection is critical. On a 1 to 5 scale, Apex Eclipse has to rate a 5 in the area of IP, which would fall within the company's asset base dimension. If Apex Eclipse is a little weaker in other dimensions, that won't affect the hunger for its technology in the marketplace. Someone will pay a premium price for Apex Eclipse, even if the company doesn't have any more products in the pipeline or its sales force consists of two more eighty-five-year-olds plucked from a retirement home. Apex Eclipse will get its premium valuation.

Conversely, another company produces generic pharmaceutical products for Walgreens, Savon-Osco, and other big drugstore chains. It makes the house-brand milk of magnesia, Pepto-Bismol, and other such products. For this company, success isn't about intellectual property. There is more to the business than going on the Internet and pulling down the recipe for generic milk of magnesia, but it's not impossible for somebody else to build a factory, figure out the recipe, and compete.

This company has to be a 5 on a 1 to 5 scale in terms of efficiency, which falls within the dimension of business management. It simply has to be better than the competition—much better—at producing these products in the most efficient, cost-effective manner possible. Does it need to be strong in IP to build premium value? Of course not. These are generic products. Does it need to have an off-the-charts research and development team? No again. The company's advantage comes from its ability to produce those products in the most efficient manner possible. Its operational efficiencies carry it to the premium-value level.

Another example has to do with the leadership, management, and culture dimension. Microsoft bought a company called Groove in 2007, not because Microsoft was in love with its products, but because Groove happened to have Ray Ozzie on its management team.[20] Ray Ozzie is a rock star when it comes to technology development, having developed Lotus Notes software in the 1980s.

Microsoft didn't care at all about how well Groove was managed and may not have cared much about what products or services it was developing or what kind of asset base it had. Microsoft bought the company because it wanted Ozzie. It paid a premium to get him, but I'm sure it still considered that price a bargain.

The Eight Internal Dimensions of the Enterprise Value Drivers

A closer look at each of the eight internal dimensions of the enterprise value drivers in table 5.2 reveals that they are the in-house items you can control. They make your company what it is. After you learn about these internal drivers, you and your team will rank the six to ten areas within each dimension on a scale of 1 to 5, and at the end of the exercise you will score each dimension by averaging all the area ratings. After you tally the numbers and arrive at an average for each dimension, you'll know how leaders rank your company's performance right now.

These ratings are important because they give you a baseline and some clarity about which TIs you need to focus on. And, equally important, the ratings also provide a way to begin your company-wide conversation about what's really going on.

Table 5.2

Internal Enterprise Value Drivers

Value driver	Areas of focus
Financial performance and management	Forecast, predictability, controls (auditability), tracking, realization, and trending of revenue growth, gross margins, profitability, A/R, and A/P. Other important financial indicators: cash position, capitalization, and contract backlog. Finally, definition and tracking of key management indicators: revenue/earning per head, utilization, and bill rates.
Corporate structure, ownership, and legal	Ownership structure and legal form, including incentives and agreements. Boards of directors/advisors, including structure, makeup, role, governance, outsiders, etc. In the legal area, contracts, lease agreements, etc.
Asset base	Assets under ownership of company in terms of intellectual property, real estate/buildings, equipment, and facilities.
Product/ service development	Definition of current and roadmap of future products and services, along with the product/service development process and the management and quality of such processes.
Delivery	Process, management, and quality of the delivery process, including the installation and customization of product and service offerings.
Business management	Procurement, inventory management, and partnerships; project, process, quality and risk management; operations and distribution, efficiency and effectiveness; periodic business reviews.
Information systems and Internet	Use of information systems and the Internet to support the business internally and externally.
Leadership, management, and HR	Management structure, ability, and depth/experience of the management team and the leadership development program in place. Recruitment, retention, salary, incentive, and satisfaction levels of employees and use/management of subcontractors. Corporate culture/climate, including the level of community involvement and social responsibility the company demonstrates.

The first dimension on the worksheet is financial performance and management—how the company is doing and how you monitor it. The second dimension—corporate structure, ownership, and legal—addresses the structure of the company's ownership. If your company's equity structure looks like a family tree and you are beginning to consider an exit, it can be awfully hard to sell your company. The third dimension, asset base, deals with what the company owns. That's the intellectual property of the organization.

The dimension of product/service development addresses what products you offer and the potential you have in the products you are going to offer next. Are you continuing to build products and services that can be taken to market? When you put your company up for sale, prospective buyers will want to see its current and future road maps. They will want to know what you've got in the pipeline.

Next you and your team will rate your company in the area of delivery. Can you take your product to market? I worked with a company that created a great software product that, unfortunately, couldn't sustain itself due to delivery problems. The product needed ten engineers to install it. The company would make a sale and send out its team of ten, and then it would have to wait until those ten engineers were done before it could sell to another customer and send its engineers to their site. After a while, the whole sales model started to crumble. As Geoffrey Moore puts it, that product didn't cross the chasm.

After you've finished rating your company on the delivery dimension, you'll rate your company in the dimension of business management. If you're operating a company that moves a lot of product in and out of Wal-Mart or Kmart, then your business management has to be efficient. That's going to be your stock in trade. Rich Gergar, the founder of G&G Outfitters, has led his company to the top one-tenth of 1 percent of the thirty thousand companies that are in the $18 billion corporate apparel business. He accomplished this by being very clear that the company must be operationally efficient to make money. He and his partner, Doug Gardner, know they have to continue to improve everything the company does and constantly track its progress. They are willing to kill a bad idea when the "juice isn't worth the squeeze."[21]

On the other hand, this is an issue that wouldn't matter for Apex Eclipse because the company wants to license technology and not move a lot of product through big-box stores. But if you make products for a living, your company needs to have a solid business management dimension in place. That's true not just for the day you actually sell the company, but it's true for right now, to have the most successful business.

Information systems and the Internet make up the seventh dimension. Both of these areas are concerned with whether your company can leverage its technology. Are you making good "make or buy" decisions about what systems you're using on the inside? Are you leveraging outsourcing for systems development? Are you leveraging the Web?

The eighth and final internal dimension rates your company's leadership, management, and HR. This includes HR systems like professional development, promotion, and pay. One of the big differences in the leadership of midmarket, privately held companies and the leadership of publicly traded companies is the succession planning process. If your company is like most midmarket companies, its leaders rely on personal relationships rather than objective analysis when they decide to promote someone to the executive ranks. Keep in mind that although Uncle Charlie may be a great guy, he may not be suited for the executive suite.

Now that we've reviewed all eight dimensions for the internal value drivers, here are a few examples that illustrate areas where companies commonly run into trouble. The examples deal with companies that were preparing to make an exit, perhaps not imminently but eventually. You're beginning the process of building enterprise value, not planning an exit, but these examples are important because they show you how to view your business through the eyes of the marketplace. In these cases, the marketplace is a potential acquirer.

A big stumbling block that companies face when it comes to driving premium value is corporate structure and ownership. For example, companies that still have friends and family on the board may be looking for trouble. Or some board members may have alternative agendas. Perhaps they're not very focused on the company to begin with. Some don't know how to provide governance, they just rubber-stamp whatever decision the CEO makes because he's the person who put them on the board in the first place. Maybe they just like to go to resorts for board meetings four times a year and play golf! Companies struggle in defining their purpose and direction, and as a result they linger with a subpar valuation.

Companies with an unusual structure also can be hard to sell. For instance, one company in the defense industry was defined as a "hub zone company" because it operated in an economically depressed area. But it didn't have its defense facilities in the hub zone. Instead, it owned a cleaning service and a jewelry business in the hub zone—just so it could keep its certification. No one is going to buy a company organized like that.

Similarly, any company that bases its business development on having some sort of preferred status—like minority-owned, women-owned, or even Arctic slope businesses—will run into trouble. ("Arctic slope companies" is a distinction Congress invented for native Alaskans.)[22] While it's important that everybody gets a chance to compete, these distinctions make the waters a little murky when it comes time to sell. Financial people discount any business won with a special status. Companies like this have subpar valuations because it would take too much effort to maintain that privileged status if they were owned by a larger enterprise.

Many companies' organizations and structures spell trouble. For example, one company develops "force protection" software, or software that connects to sensors that can detect radiological, biological, or other threats. These sensors could be installed in a harbor or outside a military compound and provide a great service.

It sounds like a great company but here's the problem: the company sold its software through the sleazy world of congressional earmarks, which are essentially sweetheart bills, or clauses in bills, that Congress passes to benefit businesses in their districts. The company was able to make good earnings from those earmarks, but the future of its business pipeline is not certain and cannot be repeated. Few well-run companies, even if they are interested in getting into that market, would be willing to take on the risk of buying such a personality-dependent company, and those that would be interested want to pay a subpar price.

If you've got too many of what investment bankers call "ornaments on a tree," you've got trouble as well. For example, let's say Aunt Betty owns stock options because she put up the $50,000 that kept the company from going belly-up six years ago. But those options entitle Aunt Betty to buy stock in the company that issued it when there is a market for the stock, which is normally when a privately held company is sold. In most cases, Aunt Betty will make out great because she will have bought low and sold high, but investors find it more difficult to deal with many Aunt Bettys than one principal shareholder. If many of these relationships exist, they make it hard to complete a transaction.

Also, if the equity is spread too widely, that can make the transaction more challenging. It's important for a company to have a clean look and feel. You've got to know where your company's equity is located, and you've got to know what your board is doing.

Now you're ready to rate your company on these internal factors using the scores to fill in the spreadsheet in table 5.1. You're going to enter numbers for the first eight of the fourteen different dimensions. These are the numbers you're going to attach to the various aspects of your business.

To help illustrate how the process works, I've filled in this worksheet as an example. Notice that the leadership, management, and HR value dimension score is the average of the scores given for the areas—a 3.2 on a scale from 1 to 5.

Note: The value dimensions are made up of three to ten "areas." During an actual value-building workshop, the spreadsheet the participants use has more areas that are filled in. The score that ends up being calculated is the average of all those areas.

After you arrive at an average rating for each dimension, you'll plot these numbers on a contour map like the one in figure 3.3. Typically, these figures look a little lopsided. That's to be expected: your company can't be all things to all people; you just have to push it toward 4s and 5s in the areas where your company competes. That's what drives a premium valuation.

Once you've got the numbers, you should compare your company with your competition, which is easy to do. You can look at information gleaned from Securities and Exchange Commission (SEC) filings as well as publicly available market information to learn how publicly traded companies in your company's market function.

Then you should discuss your findings with the entire team and focus on where their scores align and where the rankings vary widely.

Most of the incremental changes that a company needs to make in order to add value take place on the internal side, and the evaluation of your company's internal drivers will help focus your efforts. Improving invoicing efficiencies, tweaking the way your information systems track inventory, or revamping your employee review process may not be the type of changes that get your company written up in the trade journals, but these small changes all move your company toward a premium valuation.

The Six External Enterprise Value Drivers

On the other hand the public accolades and recognition generally come from the external drivers. Now it's time to pay attention to the external areas from which your exponential growth will spring. The external drivers are shown in table 5.3.

Table 5.3

External Enterprise Value Drivers

Value driver	Areas of focus
Markets and marketing	Market landscape and segments, including definition, CAGR, and total available market. Includes market dynamics/trends and competitive landscape. Finally, the lead generation model is also covered in this area.
Sales and channel management	Business development practices, direct versus channel sales programs, proposal management, sales life cycle definition, sales support, and timelines.
Product/ service offerings	Breadth and depth of product and service offerings. In this context, a product offering might include software, reports, publications, databases, etc. In the real world of services, they are typically delivered by people and involve core competencies, staff skill sets, tools, and templates.
Pricing	Pricing models, strategy, and competitive pressures.
Customer base	Number of customers, concentration of customers, historical growth of customers, account management strategy, customer intimacy, retention, expansion, and satisfaction levels, including referenceability.
Customer support	Customer support function, including returns management, defect management, and automation.

The first external driver concerns markets and marketing. Do you know what marketplace your company is in? A lot of company leaders don't. For example, company leaders may say yes to an opportunity to get a contract even though the work they're taking on may have nothing to do with the core strengths of the company. They have come across a "bluebird" or a sales opportunity that falls in their lap and represents a chance for easy revenue. Suppose a company sells relationship management software in a market segment relating to associations. The company knows how to serve associations. Then it hires a new salesperson who has a background in pharmaceuticals, and suddenly it sells software to a pharmaceutical company. If company leaders do not make a conscious decision to break into an extremely lucrative market, if they're working in a market segment they don't really understand, that's dangerous. When companies work in segments other than their core market segments, it's difficult to support, it's difficult to make money at it, and it's difficult to repeat the business, all of which means that they're not only failing to add value, they're actually creating what Geoffrey Moore calls bad revenue in his book *Crossing the Chasm*.[23]

Business cases like these illustrate why any discussion about markets and marketing should start with the questions: Do you know what marketplace you're in? Do you know what segment you're in? Does it have growth potential? Who is your competition? How well known are you? If you're in one segment and you're planning to move to another, do you have a plan in place for the transition?

Because this is a complex dimension, there are many other questions to consider: Do you have a brand in the marketplace? Are you aware of it? Do you know how to leverage your brand within each market segment into which you sell? In order to create value, you've got to be known for something, you must have repeatable processes in a market segment, and you must know how to market to that market segment. In order to achieve premium value, you must have a repeatable process, a real methodology, a real way of going to market, a real value proposition. Does your company have those?

The second external dimension deals with sales and channel management. Ray Lane, the former president of Oracle, said it: "Whoever has the best channels—wins." Sometimes it can be tough to find partners, so you need your own sales force. Other times, firing your sales force and going back to relationship selling with partners is the appropriate move. For example, a company had a sales force that was great at selling features and benefits but was unable to show prospective clients that the company's product could solve their business problems. In that case, sales management didn't mean improving the sales force, it meant letting it go—as in firing it. Instead of getting into a features and benefits battle with Microsoft or IBM, the company went back to using its product to solve critical business problems. The company would always lose a shootout over how to sell features and benefits, but it could do a relationship sell better than anyone.

There are other issues to consider in the dimension of sales and channel management: How do you maintain your current customers? How do you maintain relationships with your customer base? Are senior leaders building up relationships as your clients' trusted advisors? Your goal is to be part of your clients' year-end planning. Your objective is to get to the planning table with your customers. If you can do that on a regular basis with a lot of your top clients, you're creating real premium value.

Now is the time to address your products' maturity, the third external dimension. What kind of training do you offer? What kind of integration do you provide—what else goes along with your product? Do you provide service for the product over time? Do you offer published reports? What differentiates your offerings from everyone else's? Can any other products be bolted on or added on?

Ron Jones, the former strategist and head of mergers and acquisitions for Veridian and now president of Technology & Systems with

Global Strategies Group, is a former Marine and a heavyweight boxing champion. His advice to company leaders who want their companies to be acquired is this: put your company in the critical path of the bigger companies in your niche. In other words, by looking at the big companies in your company's space and figuring out what the connection is between what your company can offer and what the big companies need, you can put your company into their critical path. To change the metaphor slightly, the large company will have no choice but to come down and scoop your company up.

Remember Stan Sloane, the CEO of SRA who made six acquisitions in three years? What did he look for in small companies that made them attractive acquisition targets? He said that their financials must be accretive. There can't be a drag on cash flow. But the real question is, Can the acquirer take your one and its one and make three? Is there really a synergy between what the acquirer does and what the target company—your company—does? Can the whole be greater than the sum of the parts? If so, that creates a very attractive target for someone like Sloane.

The next external value driver you will evaluate concerns pricing. Do you have a conscious methodology for pricing or is it the business equivalent of sticking a wet finger in the air? Companies whose products command premium pricing have a unique product that will pass the test of time. Many companies ride a wave or a bubble in market pricing and have trouble sustaining premium pricing when the market shifts, becomes mature, or the bubble bursts. When I went to work for CTX, it was an $8 million company with 3 percent earnings. By the time I left, our revenues were $20 million, and it enjoyed 8 percent earnings. But then I went to Canal Bridge Consulting; its revenues were $5 million and its earnings were 33 percent. That meant that Canal Bridge made more in earnings on the $5 million of revenue than CTX made on its $20 million in revenue. Obviously, if you've got a premium product and you manage to command premium pricing consistently over time, the market is going to value you very favorably.

An off-the-charts example of premium product pricing is Facebook, whose valuation today is approximately a hundred times annual revenue.[24] Facebook provides an excellent example of a company that commands premium pricing because it has the eyes of 70 million (and counting) users, and it is one of the most popular destinations on the Web. That dedicated user base, though at times fickle, caused Microsoft to shell out close to $250 million for less than 5 percent of the company's shares.[25]

Premium pricing also happens closer to home. For example, Starbucks charges four bucks for a cup of coffee. Is it really better than Dunkin' Donuts' coffee? The reality is that the market looks more favorably on Starbucks than on Dunkin' Donuts because Starbucks has the mysterious ability to charge much more money for the experience of a high-end or gourmet cup of coffee, even though any honest coffee drinker, if you can find one, will tell you that Dunkin' Donuts' coffee tastes just as good. But customers don't get the same high-end experience when they go into a Dunkin' Donuts shop, and that's what they are paying for. Even with slight fluctuations in the market, Starbucks still rates top dollar prices. Premium product? Debatable. Premium pricing? Believe it.

The next dimension you will address is your customer base. Think about the following questions: How many customers do you have? How wide is your base? Is your customer base so narrow that you are single-threaded into a customer that could be wiped out by a regulatory issue? Are you in a hot market or a dead market? If you are serving aging baby boomers, you're in a hot market. What kind of market are you in? Can you go visit your customers? Do they know your name?

Or is what you sell a commodity? Web-based businesses usually don't shine in this area. If you're selling millions of little products at $19.95 each, and you have demonstrated your ability to do that for a period of years, that's great. That's not easy to do. But you create more value for a company when you know your customers personally, and they know you. Let's say your company offers high-end products that cost $25,000 to $50,000 a year. As a result, it has built relationships with the CIO of Bank of America and a dozen other Fortune 100 companies. From a value-building perspective, these relationships are invaluable. They allow a strategic buyer to say, "If I buy that company, its customer relationships will allow me to sell my financial management packages into its customer base." In other words, you're giving a potential buyer for your business a whole lot of warm call contacts as part of the package. This is a force multiplier, an enormous leverage point. So as you go through the process, always ask: How well does your leadership team know your company's customers, and how well do your customers know your leadership team? The better they know you and your staff, the more value you're potentially adding to your enterprise.

The final dimension to evaluate concerns your customer support. What do you do to maintain your customers? How do you keep them happy? Is every customer a nightmare to satisfy? During the due diligence process, a prospective buyer will talk to your customers. The buyer will want to know if you have a process to support customers or if you just have people in "hero" mode fixing problems as they go. They're going to want to see an automated process and not a group of employees wearing blue tights and red capes.

These are all of the external value drivers. If you have others to add, you can put them in the place of "dimension x" and "dimension y" on the worksheet. Now rate your company on these external drivers and plot each dimension on an external contour map like the one in figure 3.4. How does your company measure up on this list?

Once you've addressed these categories, you are ready to move on to the next step. It's time to achieve full commitment from your company's leadership in order to build value in your enterprise.

CHAPTER SIX

Committing to the Process

One morning, a debate broke out on a farm. The debate was raised between a hen and a pig. The topic of the debate was "Involvement Is Equal to Commitment." The hen argued, "If someone is willing to get involved, that means he is ready to commit."

The pig said, "No, I don't think so. Getting involved is far from ready to commit."

As they were arguing and it seemed no one could totally convince the other, they heard the voice of the farmer's wife, "Honey, what would you like for your breakfast? Ham, or egg?"

The farmer replied, "I prefer ham."

Then the pig told the hen, "You see, when you lay an egg, you are involved in the breakfast. But when Farmer Jones and his wife have ham and eggs for breakfast, I am committed."

TRADITIONAL

Nothing gets employees' eyes rolling like a CEO returning on Monday morning from a management seminar with a brilliant new initiative by which the whole company will now be run. If you're going to get your company truly committed to the idea of building enterprise value, you've got to get buy-in from everyone on board. Everyone must share the vision, so you have to find the algorithm for convincing really good people that they want to be part of this process. How do you, as a C-level executive, create a sense of shared ownership with the entire leadership team? How do you get heads bobbing over this methodology for building value, so that all the thought and planning that went into the questions discussed at the off-site meeting actually come to fruition?

Making the Commitment

Commitment is actually threefold—it's emotional, intellectual, and spiritual (see figure 6.1). Most people don't do anything unless they feel emotionally connected to the process. They don't get married, buy a car, take a job, run a marathon, have a child, or do anything of importance without first having an emotional commitment to the process. People may intellectualize and rationalize 'til the cows come home, but they don't do anything unless they have a gut-instinctual, emotional desire for doing it. So before you start marshaling arguments and compelling intellectual reasons for making changes, concentrate on getting emotional buy-in first. Keep in mind that your staff and fellow executives are emotionally committed to doing things the way they've always been done, and they will use their powers of reasoning to swat away your brilliant new initiatives. What do you reach for first, their hearts or their minds? Without question, you should appeal to their hearts. Otherwise, their minds will be your worst enemy.

Making Change

Why do you make a change? Because you have to. You recognize that the market is changing, the regulatory climate is changing, environmental rules are changing, overseas markets and competition are changing. You're ahead of the curve and you see that change is inevitable, so you want to position your company properly for the future. Base your initial approach to your team on the emotional

Figure 6.1

Making the Commitment

realization that if you don't act, the company is not likely to survive. In his book *Only the Paranoid Survive*, Andy Grove tells the story of his career at Intel and writes about "strategic inflection points," a fancy way of saying "big change." According to Grove, the very best leaders see these big moments of change coming in the distance, whether they are changes in the marketplace, changes in consumer interest, regulatory changes, or some other change that will affect their businesses.[26]

Good leaders can tell when they are in the middle of such a big change. Most leaders, however, only recognize one of these changes after it's already gone by. Your job is to anticipate and define the coming change that's dictating your need to create more value in your company, and then help everyone else on your team understand and feel the importance of rising to the challenge. Mac MacLure is the CEO of RWD, a $190 million technology and training company. He says he always struggled with the emotional aspect of getting buy-in when he wanted to take this company in new directions. He recognized that working for a training company didn't exactly motivate his employees the same way that working to save lives under the direction of a Mother Teresa might have, so he would co-opt the values of his clients. One of his clients was BP (formerly British Petroleum). MacLure would tell his team, "We have to build better training systems because our training systems save lives in the regions around the world where BP does business." When his client was a major hospital, MacLure conveyed to his team that if they built a better training program, they would make this hospital, and potentially many other hospitals, safer, more efficient, with less waiting, more sick people being cared for in a safer manner, and so on. Co-opting the values of his clients and showing his team members the ultimate social importance of their work gave them the emotional leverage they needed to connect emotionally with his vision for the future of the company.[27]

When you ask Len Moodispaw, CEO of KeyW Corporation and former CEO of Essex Corporation (recently acquired by Northrop Grumman) how he created alignment with his leadership team, he'll tell you his people have a real passion for serving their customers. You see, his customer is the United States National Intelligence Community, the group chartered to keep us safe and warm. Moodispaw's leaders long ago bought into the mission, vision, and purpose of their customers, so even if parts of their jobs are boring and mundane, when they see a change coming in the customer base, they easily get all charged up about it and turn the company in that direction.

Change Is Emotional

The only way to get a team to buy into change is to start with the emotions. When team members have an emotional connection with what you are proposing, then, and only then, can you turn to the intellectual phase of the buy-in process. Now you can appeal to the engineering crowd in your enterprise. You can back up your rhetoric with spreadsheets, charts, graphs, whatever factual information they need to feel comfortable. Muster your data and show your team that buying in makes sense, not just in the heart, but also in the head and the balance sheet. A smart approach here is to purchase research from independent companies like Forrester Research or the Gartner Group, good tools that CEOs can use, depending on their market segment.

Building a Legacy

Once you've got them open on an emotional level to making the change you wish to pursue, and you have them satisfied from an intellectual perspective that your approach makes rational sense, it's time to convey to your leaders the spiritual or legacy aspect of the work at hand. This concept can be explained using the story of a man who passes three ditch diggers working in the hot sun. He asks the first ditch digger what he's doing.

"I'm earning twelve bucks an hour," he says.

He turns to the second ditch digger and asks the same question.

"I'm digging a foundation," the man replies.

He asks the third man what he's doing.

"I'm building a cathedral," the man explains.

Everyone has heard this parable in different versions, and the reason the story is so important is that it illustrates the point that our attitude about what we do dictates our ultimate level of success. As Zig Ziglar says, your attitude determines your altitude.[28] When you want to achieve this third level of buy-in from your team leaders, it's time to appeal not to their emotions or their intellect but to their sense of themselves as contributors and to the legacy they are seeking to build for themselves. Years from now, their grandchildren will ask, "We were studying the early part of the twenty-first century in school, and we learned that it was an incredible time in American business. How did you contribute?"

You want to make your team members conscious of the fact that they are not just digging a ditch but they are instead creating a legacy and not just for you! Obviously they have to see their own success in the work that they are accomplishing, or it's simply not fair to expect them to throw themselves into it body and soul. This is why World Series rings are given not just to the winning players in the starting lineup but also to the bullpen catcher, the coaches, and everyone else who made a contribution to the winning team. Everyone wins or no one wins. Have your team members ask themselves, What do I want my legacy to be? What am I contributing? How much of myself do I give to my work?

A CEO never flies solo. And a CEO never accomplishes much in terms of building value in an enterprise unless she demonstrates to everyone on the team why building value is a good thing and why it will mean something specific to them. The equivalent of World Series rings in the business world are promotions, raises, new responsibilities and possibilities, stock options, and other rewards. What are you offering to your people who succeed? How do those rewards translate into the legacies you team members envision for themselves?

The way to achieve this more spiritual level of buy-in, to get people motivated to succeed because it is the right thing to do, is to create a line of sight between the actions that your company will take over the next few months—the transformational initiatives you will be unrolling—and the overall purpose of those TIs for the company. People have to see that the path to the personal success, satisfaction, and fulfillment they seek runs through those TIs and that by focusing on the TIs, they are actually focusing on improving their own futures. Avoid confusing the concept of increasing enterprise value with the concept of exiting. Keep the focus on building enterprise value. If you do that, you can always exit if you want to. But if you're talking about exit strategy, then you'll find that many of your best employees will fashion exit strategies of their own, months or even years before you want them to leave. There's no better way to foment crisis and turmoil in an organization than to give the staff the sense that management is trying to get the company ready for sale. Employees convince themselves that they know what happens when a company is sold—half of the people are fired and those survivors are forced to fight with the employees of the acquiring company to keep their jobs. Nobody wants to go through that, so get people excited about building value. A rule you may want to consider is to never use the word "exit" before five o'clock. Anything to do with exit strategy or planning takes place after hours, so that it doesn't scare the troops. During regular business hours, make sure that building enterprise value is the goal because it is the one that everyone shares.

It's also easy to fall into the trap of only working on the fun initiatives, like making more sales calls or dreaming up new products or spending more money in research and development. Those actions may be enjoyable, but are they really adding value? If they are, then the key indicators by which your company runs will almost certainly be heading upward. When you create efficiencies through the value-building process, it's like a booster shot for your entire enterprise. This part of the process is not about making incremental change. This is not the time to ask questions like, Should we be making 3 percent more of our XYZ product than we did last year? This is the time for asking whether you should be in the business of making that product at all, or whether there's a way to put the creation of that product on steroids and make it take a huge leap forward. Above all, it's about integrating the value-building process into your normal planning cycle. You need to layer a new level of planning—a very exciting level—on top of the planning schedule or rhythm that your company already has. It's always important to remember that exits don't always happen when expected, and the world's worst situation is when you didn't run your business properly while working on your exit.

If you've got your leaders emotionally involved with the idea of building value; if you've got them intellectually satisfied that the change makes sense; and if you're able to appeal to their values and their spirituality by showing that their contributions will benefit them personally, the enterprise, and others; then you ought to have smooth sailing as you transform your company's future—and your future, as well.

CHAPTER SEVEN

Increasing Operational Effectiveness

You've got to think about big things while you're doing the small things, so that all the small things go in the right direction.

ALVIN TOFFLER

Managers must clearly distinguish operational effectiveness from strategy. Both are essential, but the two agendas are different.

MICHAEL E. PORTER

Incremental improvement gets you to par value, but not to premium value. Ron Jones, while senior vice president of corporate development for Veridian, oversaw the company's revenue growth as it exploded past $1 billion before it was acquired by General Dynamics at a premium valuation. Jones, now the president of the Technology & Systems division of Global Strategies Group and the architect of a number of successful midmarket growth strategies, says that "improving daily operational performance is necessary to achieving superior results, but it is not sufficient."[29] Amen to that. As you go through this process, you will see how your company can increase its operational effectiveness even as it looks toward the future to create explosive, exponential growth.

You'll need to focus on filling the holes, sealing the cracks, repairing the foundation—whatever metaphor you choose to illustrate the idea that you've got to take care of the smallest details to foster an opportunity to create big change as well. In this phase of the planning process you compile a list of operational action items that people simply need to get done. I advocate choosing tiger teams of junior managers, your next-generation leaders, who may not be involved with the planning process, to handle the initiatives that increase operational effectiveness while the senior people continue to drive the process and look at the big picture.

How the Work Gets Done—
the Organigraph

The most helpful tool in this aspect of the planning process is Mintzberg and Van Der Heyden's organigraph discussed earlier. Many of Mintzberg and Van Der Heyden's ideas are brilliant and can make a huge difference when put into use, but the organigraph, as you can see in figure 3.6, provides a method for visualizing exactly how a company runs. Each company has a unique organigraph. Creating it requires people to use the left side of their brain, the analytical side, to draw exactly what their organization's operations look like. The organigraph addresses environment, structures, relationships, and how the company's processes really work. It's all about drawing a work flow of how work gets done in the company.

Sometimes the actual path that people, ideas, processes, and goods and services take varies from what people, organizational charts, or company policies and procedures dictate. When the University of Maryland reconstructed the big quad opposite McKeldin Library, it installed a huge, grassy, open area. For a long time, there were no sidewalks. The planners allowed the students to wear their own paths from building to building, and when it was clear where the students tended to walk, then the planners laid down pavement, instead of forcing the students into a specific predetermined pattern.

Just as the students created their own logical paths around the campus, organizations develop a logical flow of how work gets done in organizations. Companies often have secret mechanisms that circumvent laborious processes that don't actually serve any specific purpose. Perhaps there is a process for expense account approval, but everybody knows you go to Mary in finance, and she fast-tracks your expense account for you. When I was at Boeing, the employees had large three-ring binders called "Policies and Procedures," informally known as "Pols and Pros." These rules were routinely ignored. We would check boxes on forms to indicate that we had followed the Pols and Pros, but we never did. Instead, we took a real-world approach, one that didn't necessarily match up with the approach the procedures and policies required.

Here is another example. When Paul Silber was the CEO of In Vitro Technologies, a contract research company that sold for a premium in 2006, he was always looking for ways to make In Vitro more efficient or lean. Silber found that what had started out as the "ten commandments" of how things should work had morphed into "five hundred commandments" as the company grew. All were well-intended changes, but productivity was really starting to slow down because "how things should work" was not the same as "how things actually worked." In Vitro leaders thus had to pay constant attention to the reality of how work got done in order to meet their demanding performance objectives. Your organigraph will help you understand your company as it really is—not as it exists in documents or processes that may have little bearing in reality.

Organigraph Elements

There are six aspects to the organigraph (see figure 7.1). We'll take a look at each in turn.

- *Sets*—The sets are the really big areas that drive companies. They are called sets because they barely connect with one another.

Divisions of a large multinational corporation or practices within a professional services firm are sets. Sets in an organization normally share resources but rarely much else. For example, an IT services company determined that it had two main sets—staffing and recruiting, and business development. The company leaders realized, as they went through the organigraph process, that the company's success depended on maximizing the efficiency of those two areas. However, they also came to realize that instead of working to improve those processes, they had been working in the minutiae. They would lead huge initiatives, for example, to move staff from one project to the next or to change the benefits system. These are important items, but they're not critical, and they don't drive value. What are the sets in your company?

• *Chains*—Chains are processes that are connected or linked together—how work products, ideas, products, or services change state as they go from one stop to another within the company. The classic example of this linear connecting process is the automobile assembly line.

• *Hubs*—Hubs are coordinating centers, either conceptual or physical, where information, people, or ideas come together. They are a little like airport hubs. These ideas, concepts, products, or services might get aggregated or divided, but some transformation happens. They come in looking one way and they go out looking different. Computers can be hubs for companies that process large amounts of data, managers can be hubs in professional services firms, and buildings can be hubs for companies that manufacture and distribute products.

• *Webs*—Webs are grids that have no specific center but instead allow for a free and continuous flow of ideas and people. For companies that place a premium on intellectual capital, webs are all-important. The military has traditionally been a top-down, hierarchical structure, but it is moving to what it calls web-centric decision-making processes that permit soldiers to make decisions

Figure 7.1

Organigraph Elements

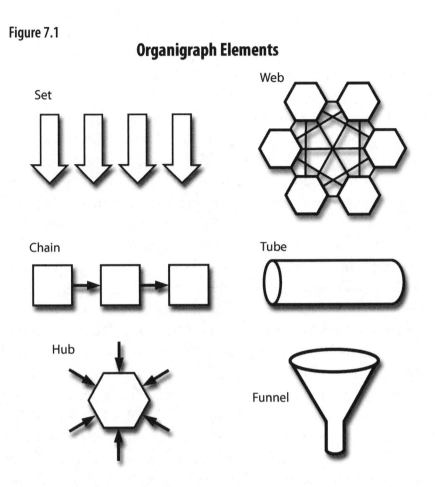

among their peers instead of going all the way up the chain of command as in the past. When you draw a web, you get to see where all the lines of communication exist in a company.

- *Tubes*—Tubes aren't so great. People, goods, services, or ideas flow or pass through tubes without any change of state along the way. Tubes usually indicate unnecessary levels of staffing or bureaucracy.

- *Funnels*—Funnels serve as filters. Funnels are where people and work get categorized, centered, or prioritized. People and information come in one end, get sorted out, and come out the other end organized in a different way.

Those are the six elements of an organigraph. Imagine a room-ful of executives when first confronted with the need to create an organigraph. You might get funny looks and rolling eyes—"Oh, no, we have to draw something." Ultimately, people have a lot of fun creating the organigraph because it provides a way to model the company without organizational charts or titles, and people don't get defensive about what they do. The beauty of the organigraph is that no feathers get ruffled. Eventually, plenty of feathers are going to be ruffled if a company has the courage to make big decisions, but through this construction, the fears and competitive instincts of team members are kept at bay while they are being extremely creative.

What comes out of the organigraph process? Two lists do: a list of what's working and a list of what's not working. To encourage discussion, I pass out three-by-five-inch sticky notes and pens and make all the participants write down all their ideas. If the ideas aren't written down, they're just a lot of hot air. But when you write them down, magic happens.

Why keep a list of what's working? Well, as the expression goes, you want to know what's not broken so you don't have to fix it. Indeed, nearly every company is doing some things right, so document those. The TIs that ultimately become selected may simply be items taken from the list of what's working and then transformed to a higher level. The process is not always about finding out what's wrong and fingerpointing. You're also trying to see what's working well and what could be working even better.

The other part of the discussion, of course, is the "what's not working" list. Invariably, this list is ten times longer than the list of areas that are working. This is a good time for people in the organization to vent or practice what I call "recreational moaning," as long as they do so in a professional manner. It's worth collecting these thoughts and then categorizing them in terms of the fourteen value dimensions, internal and external, as discussed previously. You can put those fourteen value dimensions along the walls as headings and then take the sticky notes that everybody's written and categorize them in terms of those value dimensions. This leads to important realizations about where the company actually is. You might realize, for example, that you don't have the brand recognition you might wish to have, so you can look for incremental improvement in this area.

By the end of the morning—and this whole process generally takes just one morning—you'll have ten to twenty areas where improvement is possible. Refer to this list of ten to twenty improvements as candidate TIs. In the afternoon session, which forms the basis of chapter 9, you'll pick three to four items, and those will be your actual TIs. The items left over become a to-do list for increasing operational effectiveness, and these items are typically divided up among the management team.

Increasing honesty is the hallmark of the organigraph process. Early on, you made a contour map that showed how your business looks on a 1 to 5 scale on several dimensions. Now you get to ask whether that contour map still makes sense in light of the new information revealed as a result of the organigraph creation process. For example, what if management gave itself a 5 in marketing and now it realizes that it has no brand? Obviously, there's a bit of a disconnect. Initially, company leaders want to look good as they go through the self-examination process, and they especially want to look good to outsiders like myself. But given enough time and enough opportunity for realistic thought, people become increasingly honest. Maybe marketing didn't really deserve a 5, people will admit at this phase of the process. It really just deserves a 2 or a 3. Misalignment between your contour map and your organigraph indicates that the team might not have been entirely honest early on, unwilling to face the brutal facts of where the company is in the marketplace.

The honesty is growing, the to-do list or list of candidate TIs is growing, and that's where you should be. Is this the time to start editing out some of those candidate TIs and shortening the list? Absolutely not. Your attitude should be, the more the merrier. The more items on your to-do list, and honesty in the process, the better you and your team will truly understand what drives value, where your company really is, what's working, and what's not.

Working for Hyperbolic and Incremental Growth

Ironically, this is where most planning processes stop. People look up and say, "Yep, we've got it!" and take their to-do list and bury it under a pile of file folders somewhere. That's a pity because that list of candidate TIs represents the smartest, fastest way to increase operational effectiveness and it gives you possibilities for areas in which truly transformational growth is possible as well. In his book *Mission Possible*, Ken Blanchard describes a present curve and a future curve like the ones in figure 7.2. On an X/Y axis, the present curve is a gentle slope pointing, one hopes, upward.[30] That upward tic is the gain represented by incremental growth due to increased operational effectiveness. Of course, it's the transformational initiatives that give your company that hyperbolic or hockey stick growth, so you want to have people working on both kinds of items. What's the difference between a candidate TI that increases operational effectiveness versus another one that can trigger hyperbolic growth? Using the area of financial management as an example, a company might realize as it creates its organigraph that it needs to upgrade the accounting and financial systems. It realizes it has a need for an integrated customer management system that has all the components of human resources, payroll, accounts payable, accounts receivable, and cost accounting built into it.

Figure 7.2

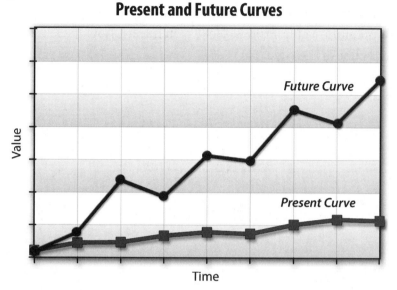

Present and Future Curves

A second candidate TI might be to recapitalize the company because its line of credit is currently too restrictive in a new market segment it is attacking. What's the difference? Upgrading the accounting and finance systems is going to take a lot of hard work. It will make the enterprise run more smoothly, but it's a foundational item as opposed to a transformational process. Recapitalizing the company, by contrast, is a big deal because recapitalizing might allow the company to expand into a whole new business area, hire a new sales staff, or do something else that will create the kind of growth that gets everybody—from management to stakeholders, Wall Street analysts to potential buyers—excited and enthused. It triggers huge growth as opposed to incremental growth.

So far the process has given you a thorough grasp on the "as is" model of your company that you need. You now have a road map to increasing operational effectiveness. Next you will create a model of where the company can be. The gap between where you are now and where you can go can be a source of frustration but it can also be the generator of the TIs that get you to that next level, the place where premium value resides. Next, you'll learn how to define that gap and choose the right TIs.

CHAPTER EIGHT

Visioneering

The greatest danger for most of us is not that our aim is too high and we miss it, but that it is too low and we reach it.

MICHELANGELO

Where there is no vision the people perish.

PROVERBS 29:18

So far, you've been focusing a lot on reality, but now it's time to move away from reality and create a new vision of the future. You want to paint a picture that gets people excited and shows them just what their company can become. You have compiled a list of up to twenty candidate TIs. The question right now is not about how to operationalize these agenda items—it's not about how many plants or how many people you'll need in order to make the simplest and most obvious (and most necessary) items happen. Instead, you want to come from the future and see just what your company can be. Later, you will worry about how to turn this vision into a reality. You cannot create a new reality until you first create a new vision.

Most organizations don't go through this exercise very often. As a result, companies frequently lack alignment between what people are doing and where they really want to go. My friend Tom Morrison, a turnaround expert currently working with Organic Alliance, created a triangle to illustrate how people share a new vision. The three points of the triangle are judgment, intuition, and action. In the center is experience. How do you get key leaders to become a part of the action? You make them a part of the process that creates the ideas that the company will implement. This is not the time to worry about turf or who gets the corner office or whether your people are making too much money. Instead, it's all about what former president George H. W. Bush called "the vision thing."[31] You need to have it if you want to go anywhere new and exciting.

Figure 8.1

Share the Vision

Intuition

Experience

Action   Judgment

Mapping the Future

John Kotter of the Harvard Business School defines leadership as a three-part process—establishing a vision, creating alignment, and motivating and inspiring.[32] Visioneering is part one of that three-step process. The Mt. Sinai approach of coming down to the people with the two tablets won't work in today's world. People must be able to identify with the vision. The best way to make a vision inclusive is to have people involved in its development.

Organizations struggle to get a shared vision of where they can go. The benefit of going through that process—it doesn't have to be a struggle, as you will see—is that it adds clarity to the values of the company. The process also defines not just where you're going, but how you're going to get there, and it is grounded in your company's values and culture. Rich Gergar of G&G Outfitters demands his leadership team get into the shoes of their customers and answer the question, What does my customer need? Clarifying these items is crucial. Not everyone may define success in the same way, but your company needs to define success in one clear, consistent fashion in order to have everyone, to use the well-worn but useful cliché, on the same page.

Your leadership team needs to have a lucid understanding of your company's core values and competencies and how exactly the company is capable of going forward. The vision needs to be stretched far enough into the future to get everyone excited, but not be so far-fetched that it starts to feel totally unfounded. In terms of thinking, encourage everyone to stretch, but at the same time there must be some aspect of practicality involved. At this point, if you have to choose between stretching and being practical, favor the stretch.

How do you know you've succeeded? Ultimately, when you present the new vision to your next-generation employees at an all-hands meeting, and you are able to get them on board, you know your vision is on target. The worst instance is when you first articulate the new vision to your people and you get a collective rolling of the eyes. In that case, you know it didn't work. The vision was a little too grandiose, a little too impractical. You have to dial it back a little bit. The vision you construct must be based on some sort of reality and not just wishful thinking. You should start communicating the vision early and do it often. Mac MacLure, CEO of RWD, meets with all new employees during their orientation to present his vision, describe his plan, and administer a "strong dose of culture."

In order to achieve not just a workable vision but also buy-in for that idea, the entire leadership team must be involved in its conception. The collective wisdom of the entire team will create a possible, practical outcome of where the organization can go. It's important to make sure that one egotist isn't dominating the conversation, grandly announcing that "we can do this" when there's nothing in the company's history that indicates that it's possible. It's also important to make sure that a diverse group of people is behind the ideas that are being promulgated. Otherwise, a big chunk of the team will be alienated.

Creating the Vision

The process by which we create the vision is similar to the organigraph process. It begins with the question, If you pick the right TIs and all the action plans get implemented the way they're supposed to, what will the organization look like in the near to not-too-distant future? As your team works on the answers, have them think two to five years out from today. I don't think there's any particular magic about three years or four years because it's very hard to have a crystal ball with that level of astonishing accuracy. Here are the other questions that naturally flow from that main question:

- How do you see your job changing? (This is a question for each person on the team.)
- Who is affected by your product or service at this point in the future?
- What are your customers doing differently?
- How has your product or service changed?
- Who is using it, and just as important, who has stopped using it?
- What new regulatory issues do you face? (The legal and environmental framework is constantly changing. For example, in Maryland, the legislature was seeking to pass a 6 percent sales tax on

technology services. Although it was eventually defeated by mid-market business leaders, this would have caused many software companies in the state to consider relocating to Pennsylvania, Virginia, or the District of Columbia had it passed. What regulatory, legal, or environmental issues will your company be facing in the future?)

- Who are the leaders in the marketplace by that future date you've chosen?
- Who's collaborating with your company?
- Who could potentially become a collaborator?
- What's the image of your company? What are all your stakeholders—your employees, your customers, your partners, your bankers, your prime contractors, your subcontractors—saying about you?
- Is there any obsolescence in the market you currently fulfill?
- Is there anything that you're doing that will go away, be done differently, be off-shored, or otherwise be unrecognizably different from its current state?
- Are the millennials, the generation born after 1984, important to you? How are you appealing to them as a service provider or as an employer?
- Do you care about your company's role in the community? Are you going green? Are you philanthropic? What does your organization care about?
- What are your unique contributions as an organization? What is your company's purpose ?
- What skills do you and your staff need in the future that you don't have now?
- How have you gotten through changing times? How did you get through the downturn or recession of 2009?
- How do you treat people? How do you recognize them for what they do? What are the core values of your organization?

- How do you retain people? The Greenbrier Resort has a wall that displays the photos of employees of ten, twenty, thirty, forty, and even fifty years' standing. The wall represents how much the culture of the Greenbrier values long-term relationships with its workers. Does yours?
- What has your company done to ensure that there is a legacy, a next generation of leaders?
- What goals and objectives would your team have after you have accomplished this current round of TIs?

It's best to discuss each of these issues over a fifteen- to twenty-minute period and give everyone the green light to say or contribute whatever comes to mind. As the expression goes, the mind is like a parachute—it works best when it's open. This process is all about opening people's minds to what the future can be.

After each of the questions has been thoroughly discussed, give the team this exercise, courtesy of my colleague Susan Stalick, author of *Business Reengineering: The Survival Guide*.[33]

On a large sheet of paper each leader must draw a map, some sort of allegorical or metaphorical construct of what he thinks the future will contain. These maps may have features like valleys, mountains, oceans, cliffs, deserts, beaches—whatever the executive wants to use to illustrate the future of the company. One map may look extremely different from another. Sometimes they look like the maps on Map-Quest, and sometimes they are maps of the galaxy, straight out of *Star Trek* or *Star Wars*. Any concept is fine as long as it represents a vision of the key features of the organization in the future time. One CEO I knew drew a mountain on his map and depicted an individual pushing a snowball that grew increasingly larger on its rise to the peak. His point was that the snowball was going to roll, one way or the other, and both directions seemed uncontrollable. How do you get a grip on that snowball before it turns into an avalanche? That's the question he wanted to think about.

Some people hate this exercise, some love it. If there are twenty people in the room, you can break them up into teams of five. Ideally, you just want three or four maps when you're done. If the group is only two or three or four people, it's harder to get everyone involved because people in a smaller group often feel more embarrassed about sharing what they're thinking about. Teams of five work out great, especially if there's an artist, real or self-styled, in each group.

Maintaining Momentum

It's also important to consider how to maintain momentum while working on the infrastructure of a company. As the expression goes, it's tough to work on a plane while it's flying. But then, you've got to consider the space shuttle. NASA is continually working on the shuttle, not only when it's grounded but also while it orbits Earth. It is possible to make small changes and even big changes while everything is up in the air, literally and figuratively.

You want C-level executives to realize that they are already paying for visionaries—they're on staff, but they may never have been listened to in the past. The employees of a $20 million technology company were finally able to get their CEO to recognize the importance of a particular new service they wanted to offer. The team said, "We've been beating him over the head for a year trying to get him to listen!" Well, he's listening now. Whether the company is too late to market is something only time will tell, but it's a certainty that this CEO wasn't paying attention to the visionaries on his own staff.

Creating a vision doesn't mean battening down the hatches to prepare for a recession. It's not about looking at the next wave and figuring out what to do. It's knowing what to do with the wave after that.

Once you have all these maps, and you have a vision of what you want the future to look like, you can begin the gap analysis. How do you get there? Going forward, you have three lists to consider—what's working right now, what's not working, and our new category, the attributes of the future. You will consolidate these lists and relabel them so that you'll have fifteen to twenty candidate TIs. Many of these candidate TIs aren't revolutionary in nature—they're simply actions that have to happen, agenda items. The challenge now is to prioritize your candidate TIs and choose the right path. Because you completed a sound analysis of your current state and have looked into your future possibilities, you can rate the TIs, looking at them in terms of risk and reward, and then determine exactly how each TI will increase the value of your enterprise.

CHAPTER NINE

Choosing the Right Path— Transformational Initiatives

Determine that the thing can and shall be done and then we shall find the way.

ABRAHAM LINCOLN

Leadership is the ability to translate vision into reality.

WARREN BENNIS

It's time to complete the gap analysis and create a list of potential transformational initiatives. The team must buckle down and make some hard decisions. It's time to move into your vision of the future. By the end of this part of the process, your leadership team will have identified the three TIs—the three changes that will really drive value going forward.

The Rule of Three

Why choose only three TIs? Why not choose seven, eight, or ten? Why not just work off the candidate TIs and call it a day? There are two reasons why you should only choose three. First, the biggest problem for many midmarket companies is a lack of focus. Many midmarket executives have so many things on their plate that they don't know where to start. If you and your team pick just three and focus on those three main initiatives, your probability of completing each and subsequently adding real value to your company goes through the roof. If you choose seven to ten initiatives, chances are that a year from now you'll still be working on the same seven or ten incomplete initiatives.

The other reason is a bit more esoteric. One of the tricks of effective communications is the "rule of three." You've heard it all your life: Life, liberty and the pursuit of happiness. Mind, body, and soul. Father, Son, and Holy Spirit. In fact, your mother probably used your first, middle, and last name when she had a TI she wanted you to work on!

As a leader, your job is to constantly talk up your three initiatives. Having just three will allow you, your team, and the entire company to focus on specific tasks, and it will help you create a shared vision for your company.

When considering which TIs to choose, start with this question: Will it actually add value to the organization? It's easy to get so caught up in the exercise that you forget the desired end result—adding value to the company, whether to achieve the goal of an exit or for any other purpose. So don't lose sight of what this work is all about—choosing the right TIs.

Think of a funnel. All of the potential candidate TIs go in, and only three or four will come out. Let's take a deeper look at the funneling process. Of the twenty or so candidate TIs you have identified, some could be bundled together with others. For example, one candidate TI might be, "Roll out a series of new products related to new research we have done." Another might be, "Resegment in the marketplace to know who's buying what." Once you start looking at these candidate TIs in terms of value dimensions, they could be seen as two sides of the same coin. Market segmentation may be a component and a product of product development, so you know what products to get into and what markets to sell into. The trick is to avoid becoming so big that when you operationalize these initiatives, they become unwieldy to carry out.

Say you were able to combine six of the candidate TIs into three new, broader TIs. That still leaves about seventeen to evaluate. The next step is eliminate the TIs the group does not believe are worth pursuing at this time. Something may be a good idea, but is it a good idea to pursue right now? If not, discard it. Perhaps that process knocks out five more ideas. Now you're down to twelve. In order to evaluate them more thoroughly, look at them in terms of the value dimensions. Are you looking at ideas that will add meaningful value, internal or external? If so, keep them in the running.

Figure 9.1

TI Rating: Impact versus Risk

Risk	Low	Medium	High	Very High
Low	Not Worth Doing	Analyze	Desirable	Desirable
Medium	Not Worth Doing	Analyze	Desirable	Desirable
High	Undesirable	Undesirable	Analyze	Analyze
Very High	Undesirable	Undesirable	Analyze	Analyze

| | Low | Medium | High | Very High |

Positive Impact

Rating Your TIs

The next method of rating the remaining candidate TIs involves positioning them according to the criteria explained in figure 9.1. In simple terms, you're looking at the candidate TIs in terms of impact and risk. You also want to study the relationships between the TIs that you choose—how well the three or four that are chosen interact with each other. First you look at impact. Impact is the likely potential positive effect on company value that may result from the successful execution of a TI. The two variables to consider here are the likelihood of something good happening and the nature of what that happy event might be. You want to create a rationale for selecting each of the proposed TIs. For example, the impact of a new regional sales model is high because creation of additional channels (a key area of sales) can potentially double sales volume in the Southeast. Big impact. You'll measure risk momentarily, but at first glance, this one looks like a winner.

For a more complete set of definitions, use the impact scale in table 9.1. The best TIs fall into the high category—they have a high potential positive impact on company value, which I define as 20 to 40 percent growth. That's good. Anything above 40 percent would be very high, and the problem with very high is that an impact that terrific is highly unlikely. You've been dreaming and imagining and creating a new future, but you have to pay attention to reality. How many things can a typical midmarket company do that legitimately boost its value in excess of 40 percent?

Whatever you decide to do is going to carry a certain amount of risk. You'll need to evaluate the risk and measure it. Risk is defined as the potential that a TI might not be successfully executed. The definitions in table 9.2 can help in your evaluation. You need to create a rationale for the risk level you assign to a TI in terms of additional resources—human, physical, capital, and money. Will

Table 9.1

Impact Scale

Potential impact level	Impact level description
Low	There is little to no potential positive impact on company value that may result from the successful execution of this TI. Provide rationale.
Medium	There is nominal potential positive impact on company value (i.e., + 10 to 20%) that may result from the successful execution of this TI. Provide rationale.
High	There is high potential positive impact on company value (i.e., + 20 to 40%) that may result from the successful execution of this TI. Provide rationale.
Very high	There is very high potential positive impact on company value (i.e., 40+ %) that may result from the successful execution of this TI. Provide rationale.

the investment of time and money as well as the opportunity cost be a risk that is worth taking? Next, talk about competencies. Do the competencies you need exist in the company? Can they be brought to bear on this TI? This is the make or buy decision.

Maybe a candidate TI deserves to be dropped from consideration because it's too complex. Perhaps it's too expensive or too far-fetched. In that case, make a conscious decision that you're not going to move ahead with that TI. You don't need any wild and crazy ideas here—you're not looking to "bet the company," as the expression goes. The ideal you seek is medium risk with high return, not something that will bring the company to its knees.

Another factor to consider is time. How much time is involved in the creation of this TI? A pharmaceutical maker might say, "We need a new product to complement our current line of generic pharmaceuticals. We need something more than cough and cold medicine. Maybe we need to go into homeopathic medicine." If you're thinking about a TI like that, you've got to quantify the time it will take to

Table 9.2

Risk Scale

Potential risk level	Risk level description
Low	There is little to no risk that this TI cannot be successfully executed. Provide rationale.
Medium	There are some risks associated with this TI and it is likely that it can be successfully executed. Provide rationale.
High	There is high risk associated with this TI and it is unlikely that it can be successfully executed. Provide rationale.
Very high	There is extremely high risk associated with this TI and it is very unlikely that it can be successfully executed. Provide rationale.

implement it and question whether it will be worth the effort later on. A change like this takes time. If you are building the creation of a homeopathic line of pharmaceuticals into your company's master schedule, will it delay other things? You want to consider not just resources to be expended but whether other things you've got going on might be delayed in a manner that is injurious to the company's growth.

You've figured the impact and created a rationale for your beliefs about the impact of a TI, and you've done the same thing for risk. So now it's time to turn back to figure 9.1. As you can see from the chart, when you place TIs on an X/Y axis, where X measures impact and Y measures risk, there are four possible results: not worth doing, undesirable, analyze, desirable.

With TIs that are not worth doing, the risk may be low, but the impact on the organization is negligible. However, something that is categorized during this phase of the analysis as one you should avoid is an initiative that may still be worth pursing as an incremental change. It is something to be assigned to a more junior team in the organization and monitored but nothing that requires the intensity of effort that a true TI demands.

Then you've got TIs that receive an undesirable rating. These are not pursued. The combination of low risk and low impact portend a waste of resources with little gain. What's beautiful about this process is that your company gets to discover in advance that a TI might fail to pay off. Typically, companies only discover this fact in retrospect. As the carpenter's old adage tells us, measure twice, cut once.

Then you come to the third category, analyze. Here, you're not making a decision to pursue or not to pursue. Instead, you are simply continuing to monitor the situation. For initiatives with high potential impact, you want to consider further exploration in order to mitigate risk. Initiatives with low risk are worth bumping down to lower elements in the organization. Here's the problem with this area: once you start telling people to rank initiatives on a 1 to 5 scale, most people give everything a 3. It's easier to take a noncommittal, bland, plain-vanilla approach to each initiative and call it a 3, but what was accomplished? Be careful about going to middle-of-the-road. Move out of the comfort zone and try to grow.

Finally, the fourth category, desirable. Pursue these. The combined high impact and manageable risk make these TIs attractive indeed. Chances are, you'll have narrowed those initial twenty candidate TIs at the top of the funnel down to just four or five by this stage. This is no time for company leaders to be gung-ho and say, "We can do all twenty!" No, you can't. That's what gets companies into trouble in the first place—branching off in too many directions with too little focus, with too few resources spread too thinly. Company leaders need to realize they are putting their money, time, and effort into changes that can make a serious difference. You and your team need to think through your bets.

Prioritize

How do you whittle those remaining candidate TIs down to three? The answer is prioritization. One way the leadership team can accomplish this is through a "dot" exercise. Each person writes his name on the dot and places it on the whiteboard next to the TI that he thinks is best. The winners are the TIs that have the most dots. Simple, but extremely effective.

While all this is going on, however, the CEO might be in the corner, quietly tearing her hair out. She's got to have veto power. She's got to be able to say, "I know you all think this is the right way to go, but I think this other way is the best way." Indeed, CEOs must have ultimate veto power because frequently they have more vision than anyone else. That's what they're paid for. The group is the group, and everybody's contribution is valued, but the CEO still sits at the head of the table.

You've chosen the top three TIs, and the CEO may be sitting impassively, but she's not turning seven shades of purple. Now ask this question: Will implementing these TIs really transform the organization? The best way to determine an answer is to redraw the contour map discussed in chapter 5.

Each TI now gets its own miniature business plan. You will decide what you're going to do in a specific time frame in order to meet a specific management need, with the goal of impacting the key management indicators you've selected while building value in the process. For example, a winning TI might be this: create a management incentive plan by June to motivate and encourage the business unit leaders to drive revenue and meet their production goals.

When you have your TI, it's time to build your TI team around that initiative. Since you'll be creating tiger teams to implement the TIs, you will want to focus on the relationships among the tiger teams, so that people are not working in a vacuum. Sometimes it's useful to plan out all of these TIs on a single master schedule, so that you know you've got to do one step before you get to the next. You will decide who the members of the team will be, who will actually have ownership of the TI, who the lead person will be to keep the TI on track, and the relationship of the CEO to the TI. Perhaps the CEO is going to serve as coach to the team members to help push this initiative through. You need to schedule milestones, determine methods of communication, and be absolutely clear on investment, risk, return, outcome, outputs, expected results, and the relationships among the TIs. See figure 9.2 to get a sense of what the initiative template looks like.

It takes the team about a week to ten days to build a business plan for each TI. The members should be very detailed regarding how the TI will actually be implemented. They identify resources and allocate people, time, and resources toward these initiatives. At the end of that seven-to-ten-day period, it's time to present the TI business plan to the entire leadership team or group staff involved in the value-building process. This is a board-level presentation, and it's got to be very sophisticated and well thought out in order to make the TI clear and compelling to everyone. At the same time, the CEO needs to make a decision regarding this TI and the other two or three that the company has chosen. She's gotten great input, excellent analysis, and a raft of candidate TIs from which to choose. Her leadership team has figured out the best three or four. It's time for her to sign onto or veto the choices the team has made, get the heads bobbing, get people moving, and get the show on the road.

CEOs need to stay on track as the TIs are implemented. Some want to look in every week, some every month—each CEO has a different way of tracking progress. Many CEOs in midmarket companies will be intimately involved in one or more of the TIs. Once you've chosen the three or four TIs, the people who will run them, and the means by which they will be implemented, you need to

Figure 9.2

Initiative

Name of initiative: _____

Initiative description: _____

_____

_____

_____

Describe initiative in terms of an action to be taken in a specific time frame to meet a specific business need with the goal of impacting a key management indicator (e.g., create a management incentive plan by June of this year to motivate and encourage business unit leaders to drive revenue and meet utilization goals).

Team:

    Sponsor: _____

    Lead: _____

    Members: _____

                 _____

                 _____

Action plan: (activity • time frame • milestone • objective)

1. _____

2. _____

3. _____

4. _____

make sure they actually happen—on time and within budget. When it comes to taking ultimate responsibility for the care and feeding of the TIs, the buck stops on the CEO's desk.

You and your team have taken a long, hard, honest look at where you are and where you want to be and now you've begun to implement the best TIs. It's time to talk about what it truly means to lead change and what a CEO's commitment to a TI can and must be. You know what you need to do and you've begun to do it. Now you've got to make sure everyone stays inspired and excited about making the TIs come true—and ultimately adding exponential value to your enterprise. The leadership piece is the one that completes the entire puzzle.

CHAPTER TEN

Defying Gravity

Gravity is a contributing factor in nearly
73% of all accidents involving falling objects.

DAVE BARRY

Heights by great men reached and kept were not obtained
by sudden flight but, while their companions slept,
they were toiling upward in the night.

HENRY WADSWORTH LONGFELLOW

Transformational initiatives are now moving forward. But are they going to succeed or will the entire process wither as many flavor-of-the-month corporate initiatives do?

If you're the CEO, the business owner, or the leader of the organization by any title, the fates of the TIs are up to you. This is where a lot of leaders falter—they've established the TIs, they've put people in place to run them, and they've got great goals. But they lack follow-through. No one keeps the commitments. This leads to an enormous amount of frustration, and it's when off-site euphoria turns into "fire the consultant." So how do you prevent this kind of unfortunate situation?

Keep Building

The leader must keep in mind the higher purpose of the entire TI process. It's about consistently building value, instead of looking at value creation as a one-time deal. The process is about aligning the people who are leading the TIs, not just with the goals of the company, but also with the other TIs, so as to ensure that when the inevitable competition for resources arises, be they financial, personnel, or other resources, everyone remains on the same page. As an organization attempts to change itself, the staff's morale and sense of purpose can get shaky, so it's all about sticking to the path you've chosen so carefully.

Creating alignment in a company during a time of serious change is something like the image that some of the large consulting organizations like to use. Think of cowboys herding cats. It's not easy! The more powerful the organization is, the more powerful the people within your organization are. And the more powerful and entrepreneurial the people within your organization are, the greater the likelihood that they are going to establish different priorities one day after the transformational initiatives have been announced.

It's your responsibility to stay on message forever and ever and to make sure that the TIs get done. Furthermore, your leaders have to trust you, because you are the keeper of the vision. Also, the leaders of the TIs must trust each other in order to implement and execute the TIs. It's easy to talk about trust, but it's hard to establish. According to statistics from Work USA 2006/2007, only half of American workers trust their bosses.[34] The figure is even lower in the United Kingdom, where it drops down to just 30 percent of employees who feel a sense of trust toward management. You're not just fighting the competition. You're fighting malaise and mistrustfulness in your own organization. Its difficult to overcome but it's doable.

Just how hard is it to attain trust? I was recently speaking with Dr. Paul Silber, the CEO of In Vitro Technologies, a company that first came to business fame by testing cosmetics in test tubes rather than on animals, as was the industry standard. He sold his company for a huge premium after having aligned his leadership team to institutionalize the concept of being a lean company. The lean buzzword refers to manufacturing, processes, and other aspects of an organization. What could be simpler or more desirable than being lean? Well, just as human beings have a tough time trimming the fat, so do companies, even nimble and forward-thinking companies like In Vitro. It actually took six months to convince the leadership of the company to go lean, and that process required consultants, assigned readings, and a firm hand at the tiller to make sure that the change took place. There's nothing easy about changing the behavior of leaders in order to get them to stick with change. You've got to find statistics, anecdotal evidence, appropriate motivational speaking, and other tools to get them on the same page and keep them there.

John Kotter published *The Heart of Change: Real-Life Stories of How People Change Their Organizations* with Harvard Business School Press in 2002 in which he talked about the need to create a sense of urgency, to develop a team to guide change, to clearly communicate the vision, to knock down obstacles, and to create and publicize short-term wins. We'll take a look at that last piece, since we've discussed in great detail all of the others throughout the rest of the book. Short-term wins get people excited. If your staff knows that good things are happening, that you've just won a big contract, that revenue is up, or whatever the short-term win might be, they'll be happy. If they don't know about those positive results, if leadership is doing a poor job of telling the team about short-term wins, then many employees will be looking for jobs. It's up to you to fill in the cracks of ambiguity that result from inaccurate information that somehow leaks into the water cooler conversation at your company. So, as the little victories occur, make sure that they are communicated—and celebrated—because many of your most important assets ride the elevator to the lobby every evening, and you want to keep them engaged.

Keep Driving

Another essential attribute of a leader who can drive change is the ability to keep one's foot on the pedal. This is where entrepreneurially minded people shine. They just hammer and hammer and hammer away, often down the wrong road, but they can self-correct. That kind of dogged determination is essential to push a TI through. A leader who is confronted with obstacles will find ways through, around, or over them. When it comes to driving change, you can't let up. The forces of inertia that are opposing you are too strong.

Suppose you accomplish something special early on through one of your TIs. As an example, perhaps you have streamlined your business development filter in one particular region to identify only high probability candidates to pursue as clients. If that worked well, institute it across the company and let everyone know of the benefits that are flowing from the TI process. You've created a new "gating" process to screen out bad prospects, and this is something from which everyone in the company will benefit, directly or indirectly.

Grow or Go

So far we've talked about the philosophy behind managing change. I call this chapter "Defying Gravity" because that's exactly what you're doing. The natural tendency of any organization over a period of time is either to level off or, more likely, to start on a downward slope. People become de-energized, good people may leave for challenges elsewhere (or simply to travel the world on their new yacht if the early days were spectacular enough). The sense of "pedal to the metal" and the initial enthusiasm often give way to institutional torpor, where work gets done, somehow, and targets are reached, if only barely so, but the fizz has gone out of the champagne. This is the natural tendency not just of a business but of almost anything in nature—a tree, a marriage, a life. Gravity pulls back to Earth even the highest of fliers. If your company is going to survive, it will do so because there will be growth. And if your company's going to thrive, it will be due to massive, sustained, exciting, enterprise-wide growth. The laws of nature apply just as firmly in the business world as they do in the great outdoors—grow or go. In business, there's one slight addendum to grow or go—it's grow a lot or prepare your company's obituary. You're not in the obituary-writing business; you're in the business of leading meaningful change. How do you get into action to make that happen?

First, it's essential to review TIs on a regular basis. You've got to be diligent about receiving regular reports, be they weekly, bi-weekly, or monthly. It's up to you to make sure that your people stay focused on the TIs with which they have been tasked. If they don't sense a continuing urgency from the top, they'll find other actions with which to occupy their time—crisis management, their own ini-tiatives, or just simply returning e-mail and running in place. Your diligence must be manifested in terms of expecting or demanding regular reports, so you know what exactly is going on. The reports should contain information about schedules, milestones, returns on investments, roadblocks, outcomes, outputs, wins and opportuni-ties. The means by which those wins and opportunities are being institutionalized should also be included in the reports. You've got to keep your finger on the pulse of the TIs, or else they may not have a pulse for long.

Second, it's important to recognize that TIs are invariably related. There will be inevitable conflicts with regard to resources. Perhaps one of your TIs calls for a change in packaging, and that in turn requires a new agreement with a sourcing company. Another of your TIs has targeted subcontracts management as a problem area and has decided to change the way all vendors are managed, so rene-gotiation of contracts is not possible with your sourcing company right now. You've got to play referee, and you've got to be able to make decisions, if not on the fly, then fairly quickly. That's because momentum is key to ensuring the health and success of a transformational initiative.

The third key involves managing the various stakeholders inside and outside of your business. The key question is this: What's in it for them? When I was at CTX, we were in the process of a management leveraged buyout that was, ultimately unsuccessful. After it failed, I left the company, and if anyone asked me why, I told him it was because of philosophical differences. It doesn't take much reading between the lines to know that philosophical differences was code for getting fired. Why? Because I hadn't paid attention to my relationship with the two original founders of the company, who were leaving the business at their own behest, which meant that they were cashing out. When you're leading a leveraged buyout (LBO), or when you're implementing any change that requires balancing interests of competing parties, you've got to make sure that each of those parties feels attended to, listened to, and taken care of. I had failed to create alignment with the two founders due to my own immaturity. I mismanaged my relationship with them, and when the deal went south, I was left in a horrible position. They couldn't trust me, and I couldn't blame them for the way they felt. I hadn't looked at the whole circle of stakeholders—I had just looked at the pieces that seemed most important to my own interests. After the LBO failed, the most important change management made was to get rid of me.

Figure 10.1 shows the leader in the center of the pie, and all the slices surrounding the leader represent the various stakeholders. You should build a pie that includes as many stakeholders as you can think of. Are you paying attention to all of them? If not, then some of them will be paying attention to you, and not in a way you might like.

Figure 10.1

Stakeholder Management

A much better-known example of a person who failed to manage her relationships with all of her stakeholders is Carly Fiorina and her HP stakeholders. I've heard her speak twice, once at the University of Maryland Baltimore County and a second time at a leadership summit, and to my way of thinking, she still doesn't understand how poorly she managed her relationship with her board of directors. When times got tough, as they inevitably will in the business world, she had no relationship with them, so they let her go. You never know which stakeholders are going to feel left out—the founders, managers, stockholders, employees, customers, suppliers, and so on. Your best guarantor of success is to maintain excellent relationships with all of them.

Watch the Dashboard

The next great tool to use when managing change is your dashboard. Your car has a dashboard—it tells you your speed, your fuel level, perhaps your rpms, engine temperature, and other important information. You only need a few key indicators in order to drive a car. When you're running a business, you need key indicators on your management dashboard. These might include inventory turnover, cash on hand, or whatever data are most important in your industry. You want to create a line of sight between your TIs and the impact they have on your dashboard gauges. Initially, the TIs might drain power, and you'll see that in your metrics. This is the time to develop strong nerves so that you can hold the course. Remember that you are building value now, which takes time, and you're not necessarily maximizing your cash flow or next quarter's profits. You're not, as the bankers might say, putting lipstick on the pig. The whole point of the TIs is to create long-term value, not to prop up your cash position to make your company look more attractive to immediate buyers. Many executives who are managing a TI process will experience a moment of panic, and the only remedy is patience. Ideally, you will have chosen TIs that offer high impact for medium risk, so keep your eye on your dashboard and your foot on the gas, because before long, you will have the kind of measurable results that take all of the mystery and uncertainty out of the change you are effecting through your TIs.

Remember, patience is a great virtue. Sometimes you get an immediate boost to the bottom line when you execute a TI. If you sell a division because it's no longer in keeping with your core business, that can have a happy impact on your cash flow. Reducing head count can have a similar effect. Typically, TIs are not "big bang" moments—but they will cause a powerful transformation of a company over time.

Keep all of this in mind as you institutionalize change in your company: Insist on regular reporting to keep everyone focused. Keep the pedal to the metal. Be prepared to referee conflicts over limited resources. Communicate to all of your stakeholders—not just some—what's in it for them and maintain healthy lines of communication with all of them. Create a line of sight between your TIs and your dashboard and don't expect a quick hit for the bottom line. It could happen, but the absence of one does not mean that your TI is failing. If anything, it means that you have chosen a TI big enough to create the kind of long-term addition of value that you were after from the beginning.

The Mind, Body, and Soul of Your Enterprise

Growth is an essential part of the survival of any organization. Just as any organism will die without growth, organizations will stagnate and eventually suffer if they are not constantly growing. But growth is the most difficult day-to-day task facing an executive. How much should you grow and in what direction? These seem to be life-or-death decisions. There are ways, however, of managing growth that achieve objectives effectively and organically.

The three parts of an organization that must experience growth, or surely they will die, are mind, body, and soul. For the organization to experience effective growth, all three parts must grow at the same time. A useful way to think about effective organizational growth is by visualizing three rocks held together by a rubber band (figure E.1). Each rock represents the mind, body, and soul, respectively, of an organization. All three must move forward at the same time, or else the rubber band will snap back, stymieing progress. In terms of your company's growth, this uneven movement leaves the company in the same position as when you started the growth initiative.

What exactly are these three aspects of your organization—the mind, body, and soul? The mind is the leadership, defined as those who make decisions, including but not limited to those in charge of the organization. Leaders of an organization are the people who are setting strategy and articulating vision and direction. Every member of an organization should be certain of these leadership qualities. There is leadership, in other words, at all levels of an organization.

The body of an organization consists of the key components of the organization's functioning—the process, structure, and even finances. The body is the guts of an organization.

Informing both the mind and the body is the soul of an organization—the corporate culture or code of ethics. Any effective growth strategy aims to move all three of these components forward in near unison if it is to be successful.

Figure E.1

Making the Commitment

Expand Your Mind

In terms of exercising and expanding the mind of the organization, the first step to growth is to critically assess leadership skills. A team-based appraisal, or a 360-degree assessment, is advisable. A 360-degree assessment is an evaluation of leadership capability in general. It addresses all classic leadership attributes, from establishing vision and setting direction to motivating and inspiring. A thorough inventory also evaluates classic management skills like controlling, monitoring, and directing. A 360-degree assessment shows the level of functioning of both the leader and that leader's circle of influence. Everyone who has influenced the leader becomes part of the assessment, from supervisors to coworkers to subordinates. It may very well be that a leader is good at certain parts of leadership—say, the intellectual or financial side—but lacks certain key qualities of emotional intelligence or vision. A 360-degree assessment allows both strengths and weaknesses to be highlighted.

It is essential that each person in the leadership group—not just the leader—move through this process with everyone in the group. A full evaluation and assessment can have profound consequences; new members may need to be added to the team to compensate for weak skills in the group, or perhaps new training of existing team members will be required. The most important part of an organization's growth is the advancement of the mind, though it cannot happen without the simultaneous growth of the other sectors.

Leadership assessment is generally very successful if it is approached enthusiastically and in an environment of trust. It can be tied to new planning initiatives and the development of stronger leadership skills. It's important to keep in mind that the identification of strong skills is just as important as the identification of weaknesses. Strengths, after all, will be your leverage points. But the assessment of all these aspects is important to understand and document and is crucial to preparing for corporate growth.

Leadership should not be a quality attributed only to a few individuals at the top of an organization. Growth becomes much easier and more effective when the ability to make sound business decisions is distributed throughout the organization. It is very useful to teach everyone in the company about the organization; when everyone knows how the business works, each employee understands her role in success and understands how her work is integral to that success. Leadership, then, becomes ubiquitous throughout the organization. If even lower management knows how everything impacts the bottom line, it will be easier to make it aware of how to be more productive and cost-effective. This form of transparency can be a huge benefit for the organization, especially when a growth initiative is seeking to change its deep-seated ways of doing things.

Share the Knowledge

Great executives share knowledge in ways that make it accessible and even entertaining for other members of the organization. They often use anecdotal, everyday stories that make it easier to understand how the organization works and how individual employees' work has an impact on an organization. In one company, the CFO entered a staff meeting and somewhat sarcastically stated that the company's average billing rate was less than the clown charged for his performance at the company's summer picnic. At the next staff meeting the CFO dressed up as clown to emphasize the issue, and while they got a kick out of it, project members also took him seriously and rallied to move billing rates above the clown's rate, adding four or five points to the gross margin and contributing to the bottom line. Higher rates were always in the marketplace; the company leaders just hadn't asked for them, and all it took was a clown costume to make the problem—and the solution—clear to the entire organization.

When sharing knowledge with the organization, it's important not to use complicated business terms like "return on investment capital." A key line to remember in this context is "turning Wall Street into Main Street." It's not just the content of a message that is important, but its medium. Effective approaches can be serious, somber, and often more humorous or relatable. In general, however they go about it, executives should drive home every day sick and tired of articulating the organization's vision. If they're not, they're not doing it enough.

Aligning the Body

When conceptualizing approaching the body of an organization, it is important to remember the image of the three rocks held together by the rubber band. An organization's body is its processes and structure—the core business processes the company needs to work well. These can range from inventory control to sales turnover to professional services delivery, to name just three at random. These processes must be looked at critically—just as the organization's leadership is analyzed—to make sure that they can handle the extra pressure of growth. Are the organization's structures aligned with the vision for the organization's growth and future? It may well be that some business transformation and reengineering are necessary to support the growth load, and it is crucial that these determinations are made before growth initiatives begin.

When changing the processes of an organization, it is also important to align those processes with one another (in keeping with the image, the little pebbles *within* the rocks must be held together, just as the big rocks are held to each other). Reorganization is not the only change that is important for the body of the organization. The elements, in other words, may be fine, but their alignment may be problematic. In that case, it is just as critical to realign things appropriately to ensure that the processes will not be overwhelmed by growth. These realignment plans require a collaborative approach. The factors that will make the organization work well should be discussed and articulated in a workshop format. This kind of change is not about one person imposing swift changes, but is about the organization itself making the change. Outside help can manage or facilitate the process, but it should not impose solutions. Internal input should be maximized.

Have a Soul

The underpinning of the mind and body is the soul, the culture of an organization. Culture consists of the norms of the organization. Though many workers may think that their workplace lacks a culture, it is crucial to remember that every organization has one. It can be quiet, or it can be an outrageous, noisy sales culture. Whatever the particular culture is, it is defined by a set of norms and behaviors, a code of what is accepted and not accepted. A culture is the glue of the organization. It holds the business together when other structures fall apart at the leadership or process level. But this inherent cultural stability can be detrimental during times of change. An effective culture comes from a sense of communal ownership that is born out of the shared conception of an organization's vision and operations—a line of sight between what happens day to day and the general performance of the organization. Such a line of sight leads to a sense that people's contributions are valued by the organization—an ownership culture in which everything is important to the bottom line. Creating this ownership culture has great value; when you think and act like an owner, you are comfortable with growth. Everyone should be thinking like an entrepreneur, a mindset in which what is good for the organization is good for the individual workers.

Useful methods and techniques exist for assessing the soul of the organization, and once this code of values is established, it should be publicized. Most organizations should have their values posted. If company values are common knowledge, tough decisions can be justified because such decisions—over hiring and firing, for instance—can be persuasively articulated when they can be connected with the organization's value system. In most organizations, codes of behavior—issues like lateness and timeliness, dress, and approach to customers—are left largely unspoken. This is a great potential problem. It is important that integral aspects of the culture be clear and documented and that new people are brought into the organization in accordance with this code. A code of values can even be used as a selling point, attesting to an organization's commitment to its customers and employees. Documenting these unspoken codes can be very effective. Keep in mind that in regard to the issues of organizational culture, if it's not written down, it doesn't exist.

The most important concepts and principles from the discussion about growing the mind, body, and spirit of the organization can be summed up with one word: trust. Trust is a mnemonic Bob Blonchek and I came up with when we wrote *Act Like an Owner: Building an Ownership Culture*. From a leadership point of view, these aspects should be set in place before any major changes are initiated.

TRUST—*Teach* as many people as possible in the organization how the organization works; make all information ubiquitous. Establish a *Reward* system to compensate individuals for their performance. Maintain *Unconditional* support even when mistakes are made during growth phases; mistakes are inevitable during periods of change, and you do not want to squash initiative by aggressively punishing people for these mistakes. *Share* as much information as possible; be as open as possible. As a leader, be *Trustworthy*; make and keep commitments. During a time of change, you need to be strong, consistent, and unambiguous from the very beginning. When the organization is transitioning, everyone in a leadership position needs to take a critical look at his skills to make sure that the skills are growing and changing, just as each person would like his organization to change. This can encompass professional development, reading, seminars, books on tape, executive peer groups, and many other strategies. The key thing to remember is this—if the organization is going to change, its leaders must change, too.

ACKNOWLEDGMENTS

There are so many people to thank and acknowledge in the process that led to this book. I have had the great pleasure to work with and learn from a great many business leaders over the past several years. Many have survived the value-building process, others have challenged me to improve the process, and still more have contributed in nuanced ways through conversations, consulting assignments, and interviews. To all, I wish to express my sincerest appreciation.

Kathy Adams and Armando Seay and the leadership team
    of RTGX, Inc.
Tom Anderson of ANI Pharmaceutical
Brad Antle of SI International
Rob Baruch of RABA Technologies
Wayne Beekman, Cary Toor, and the leadership team of
    InfoConcepts
Virginia Callahan of VA Associates

Don Charlton of Gratis Internet

Gus Cicala of Project Assistants

Bob Coleman, Joe Cormier, and Kevin Phillips of ManTech
International

Ray Dizon of the Maryland Department of Business &
Economic Development

Bill Dunahoo of Praxis Engineering

Leo Fox and Matt Wilmoth of Tenacity Solutions

Rich Gergar of G&G Outfitters

Danny Goldberger of Grant Thornton, LLP

Gretchen Guandola of KippsDeSanto Investment Banking

Ellen Hemmerley of the University of Maryland,
Baltimore County

John Hrabovsky of Med-Media, Inc.

Drew Hudson of Choice Staffing

Ron Jones of Global Strategies Group

Jeanne Kimmich, Ray Roberts, and Kathleen Lally of KSSI

Kris Kurtenbach, Terri Fuerinde Dunham, and the
leadership team of Collaborative Communications Group

Mike Lessing of ProSync

Mac MacLure of RWD Technology

John McBeth and Jim Long of NextCentury

Chris McGoff of Touchstone Consulting (SRA)

Len Moodispaw of KeyW Corporation

Tom Morrison of Morrison Partners

Brian Nejmeh of Instep Consulting

Tom Peltier of Stifel Nicholas

Paul Reichs of the Inner Circle of Baltimore

Dennis Roberts of the McLean Group

Dan Roche and the leadership team of e.magination

Phil Sahady and the leadership team of Chevo Consulting

Ray Schwemmer, Rich Havrilla, Chris Murphy, and
    Shawn Davis of CollabraSpace
Paul Silber of InVitro Technologies (Celsis)
Stan Sloane of SRA International
Norm Snyder and the leadership team of Conquest (Boeing)
Susan Stalick of KBMS Global
Tracy Graves Stevens of MSM Security
David Walker of Pangia Technologies

Special Thanks

A very special thanks goes to Brian Nejmeh. Brian is a professor of business information systems at Messiah College in Grantham, Pennsylvania. He also runs Instep Consulting, a consulting practice that helps companies create strong positions and whole products in targeted growth markets. Along with his academic and consulting work, Brian provides advisory due diligence and postinvestment services to technology investors.

Brian and I jointly engaged clients using the value-building process. Brian's contribution to the value dimension concept and his creation of the contour map has helped clients and prospects envision how their company stacks up to the competition.

More than anything, I appreciate Brian's support, intellect, candor, honesty, and friendship.

NOTES

1. Chris McGoff, interview by author, January 30, 2008, Annapolis, MD.
2. The Boeing Company, "The Boeing Company 2005 Annual Report" (Seattle: The Boeing Company, 2005).
3. Bradford Antle, interview by author, February 26, 2008, Reston, VA.
4. Russell Herman Conwell, *Russell H. Conwell: Founder of the Institutional Church in America* (Charleston: BiblioBazaar Publishing, 2007), 118.
5. J.F.O. McAllister, "The Candidate of Dreams," *Time*, March 13, 1995.
6. Bill Hybels, "A Vision to Die For" (keynote presentation, Willow Creek Association Leadership Summit 2007, August 9, 2007).
7. Patrick Lencioni, "A Summary of Why Executives Fail," in *The Five Temptations of a CEO* (San Francisco: Jossey-Bass, 1998), 113.
8. Jim Collins, "First Who . . . Then What," in *Good to Great* (New York: HarperCollins Publishers, 2001), 41–64.
9. Jack Welch, "Integrity Violations," in *Winning* (New York: HarperCollins Publishers, 2005), 120.
10. TiVo Corporate Web site, "Investor Relations, Code of Conduct, Our Values," TiVo http:// investor.tivo.com/documentdisplaycfm?DocumentID=1058 (accessed July 22, 2008).

11. Colin Cook and Don Spitzer, "World Class Transactions: Insights into Creating Shareholder Value through Mergers and Acquisitions" (London: KPMG, 2001).

12. Mercer Consulting Group, "Trans-Atlantic Mergers & Acquisitions: Review of Research Findings" (New York: Mercer Consulting Group, November 14, 2001).

13. Daniel J. Meckstroth "An Analysis of Merger and Acquisition Activity in the United States" (Manufacturers Alliance/MAPI, 1999).

14. Kate Miller, "PSINet Founder Runs Out of Luck—Company Operations," *Industry Standard*, May 14, 2001, http://findarticles.com/p/articles/mi _m0HWW/is_19_4/ai_75213341 (accessed July 22, 2008).

15. Tom Peters, *Liberation Management* (New York: Random House, 2006), 612–614.

16. Niccolo Macchiavelli, "Concerning New Principalities Which Are Acquired by One's Own Arms and Ability," in *The Prince* (New York: Alfred A. Knopf, 1922) chap. 6, 1515.

17. You can find the entire RFI or request for information at www.corsum.com or the Web site for this book, www.buildingbusinessvaluebook.com.

18. Dr. Stanton T. Sloane, interview by author, February 4, 2008, Fairfax, VA.

19. Harry B. Smith, David H. Mooney Jr., Ewanu Walter, US Patent 3,023,409, 1962, Pulse Doppler radar system, Assignee Westinghouse Electric Company.

20. Martin LaMonica, "Microsoft to Buy Groove Networks," CNet.com, March 10, 2005, http://news.cnet.com/Microsoft-to-buy-Groove-Networks /2100 -1014_3-5608063.html (accessed July 22, 2008).

21. Rich Gergar, interview by author, March 14, 2008, Lanham, MD.

22. House Committees on Government Reform and Small Business, *Alaska Native Corporations, Increased Use of Special 8(a) Provisions Calls for Tailored Oversight*, 2006.

23. Geoffrey Moore, *Crossing the Chasm* (San Francisco: Harper Business Essentials, 1991), 152.

24. Laura Locke, "The Future of Facebook," *Time*, July 17, 2007, http://www .time.com/time/business/article/0,8599,1644040,00.html, (accessed July 22, 2008).

25. Microsoft, "Facebook and Microsoft Expand Strategic Alliance: Two Companies Expand Advertising Deal to Cover International Markets,

Microsoft to Take Equity Stake in Facebook," Microsoft, October 24, 2007, http://www.microsoft.com/Presspass/press/2007/oct07/10-24FacebookPR .mspx, (accessed July 22, 2008).

26. Andrew S. Grove, "The Morphing of the Computer Industry," in *Only the Paranoid Survive* (New York: Doubleday, 1996), 39–48.

27. Laurens MacLure, interview by author, February 7, 2008, Baltimore, MD.

28. Zig Ziglar, "Attitude Makes All the Difference," in GOALS CD (Dallas: Nightingale-Conant, 2002).

29. Ronald C. Jones, interview by author, February 8, 2008, Annapolis, MD.

30. Ken Blanchard, "Redesigning the Castle," in *Mission Possible* (New York: McGraw-Hill, 1997), 25–75.

31. Mark O. Hatfield and others, *Vice Presidents of the United States, 1789-1993* (Washington, DC: U.S. Government Printing Office, 1997), 529–538.

32. John P. Kotter, "The Process of Leadership," in *A Force for Change* (New York: Free Press, 1990), 35–76.

33. Dorine Andrews and Susan Stalick, *Business Reengineering: The Survival Guide* (New York: Prentice Hall, 1994), 86.

34. Watson Wyatt Worldwide, "Debunking the Myths of Employee Engagement." WorkUSA 2006/2007 Survey (Chicago: Watson Wyatt Worldwide, 2007): 14–15.

INDEX

ABOUT THE AUTHOR

Martin O'Neill knows a lot about midsized companies, having spent much of the last twenty-five years operating, consulting to, and researching companies in this market. As a business operator, he started and sold a company, positioned another for a leveraged management buyout, and helped a third sell for a significant premium. Today, Martin runs Corsum Consulting, which focuses on one goal: helping companies build value. He is a member of the National Speakers Association and a frequent speaker and consultant on leadership, corporate culture, and building enterprise value and is the coauthor of *Act Like an Owner* (Wiley). He holds a number of board-level positions with midsized companies, sits on the Business Advisory Board for the University of Maryland Baltimore County (UMBC) Tech Center and lectures in UMBC's Entrepreneurship Program. Martin lives on the Magothy River in Maryland with his wife Denise, their three children, Jack, Liam, and Lily, and their yellow Labrador retriever, Sunny.

Services Available

Martin O'Neill speaks and consults to midsized companies. His message is powerful, impactful, and always leads to action. Martin is a principal with Corsum Consulting, a strategy and management consulting firm focused entirely on building value for companies in the middle market. Corsum advises leaders of middle-market companies on the issues that most impact their companies' performance and long-term value.

Corsum's method stresses one overarching theme—that middle-market companies should embrace a value-building model that addresses the needs, goals, desires, and responsibilities of all their stakeholders, from the founders and investors to the staff members. Their focus is helping smaller and midmarket companies think and act like their publicly traded bigger brothers. They apply a proven methodology to the most pressing challenges of management—and create strategic transformational initiatives that leaders can most influence to drive company performance and build value.

For more information, please contact us at

Corsum Consulting, LLC
Suite 323
1290 Bay Dale Drive
Arnold, MD 21012
410-757-6877
info@corsum.com
www.corsum.com